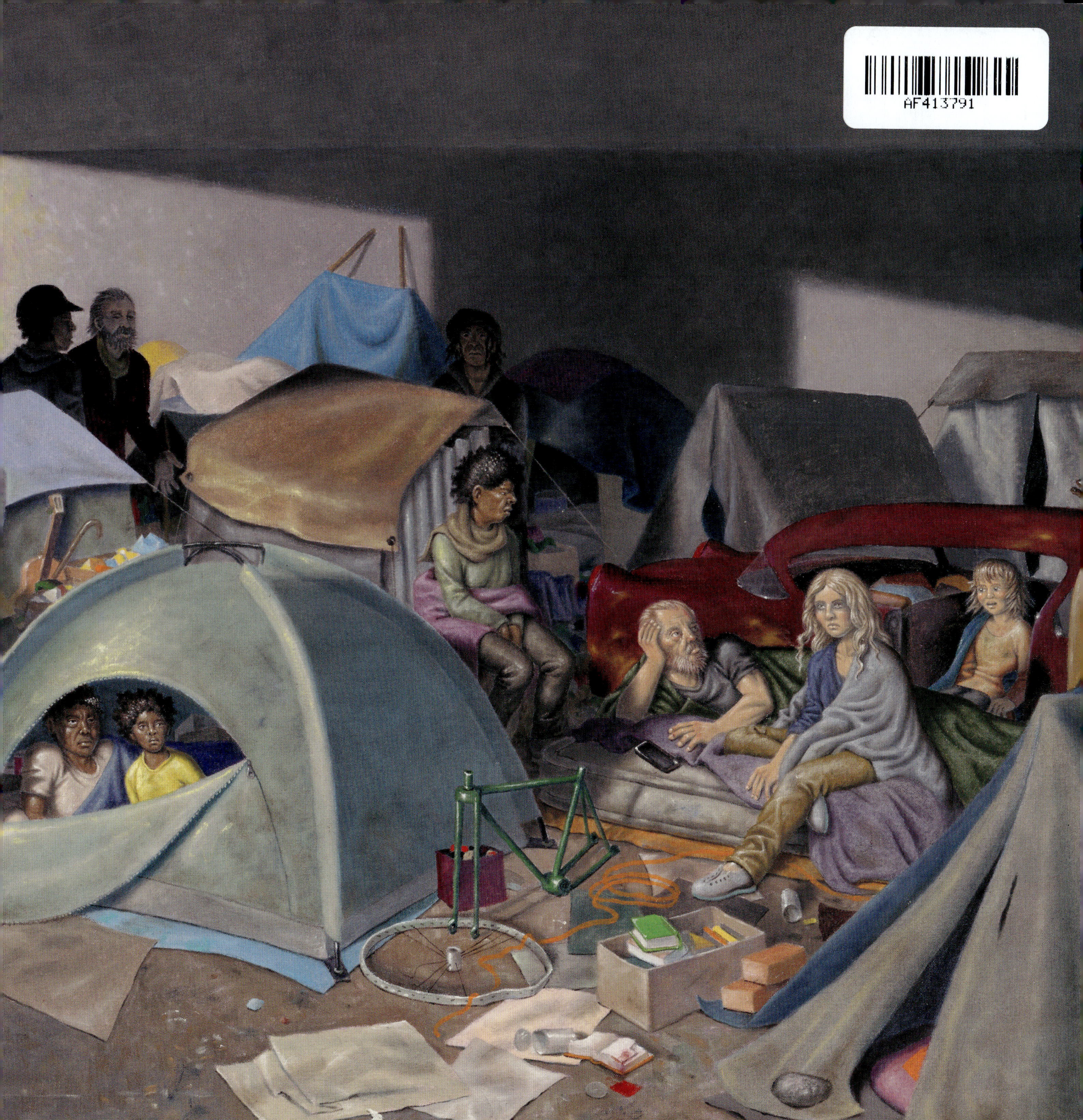
AF413791

GO FIGURE

GUY COLWELL

ACKNOWLEDGMENTS
Alex Seastrom
Julie Seastrom
Philip Seastrom
Ryan O'connor
Gary Groth
Matthew Gardocki
George DiCaprio
Ron Turner
Denis Kitchen
Fred Todd

FIND GUY COLWELL ON INSTAGRAM
@socialreally and **@inker_guy**

Supervising Editor: Gary Groth
Editor: Kristy Valenti
Designer: Justin Allan-Spencer
Production: Paul Baresh, Ben Horak
Editorial Assistance: Kenley Brinton, Cecily Greenberg, Maïa Hamilcaro-Berlin, Breelyn Mangold
Publicity: Tucker Stone
VP/Associate Publisher: Eric Reynolds
President/Publisher: Gary Groth

Fantagraphics Books, Inc.
7563 Lake City Way NE
Seattle, WA 98115 (800) 657-1100
www.fantagraphics.com

Follow us on X and Instagram @fantagraphics and on Facebook at Facebook.com/Fantagraphics

ISBN: 979-8-8750-0097-3
Library of Congress Control Number: 2024949469
First Edition: 2025
Printed in China

GO FIGURE
FIGURATIVE SOCIAL SURREALIST PAINTINGS

GUY COLWELL

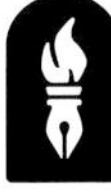

FANTAGRAPHICS · SEATTLE, WASHINGTON

MENTAL SMASHUP

Most people can recall having the experience of seeing an act of caring, kindness, love or reconciliation and feeling an urge to weep. This is a common response, yet somehow a little absurd. Why cry? Why not a sudden need to smile, break out in song or do a happy dance? It is because these acts of kindness are actually kind of strange. They are not expected. Some mental processes in the oldest parts of our brain find them incomprehensible, and they trigger a flash of cognitive dissonance in the face of something, well... not natural.

Certain instincts that have been programmed into creatures by Natural Selection may mimic altruism and caring, but are robotic executions of evolutionary instructions. It is behavior that must be performed because without it, the species would never have been preserved. It is not about actual caring.

For all of evolutionary time, what living organisms expect is to compete, to hunt and kill to eat, or to be hunted and killed. The greater part of instinctual behavior is about continuing to be alive in this remorseless reality. Watching in terror their fellow creatures being brutally killed, dismembered and consumed is the normal, natural condition of life. It is expected.

The big-brained human animal may seem to have risen a little above this tooth-and-claw existence, has begun to show small sparks of consciousness, caring and altruism. This might even suggest we have begun to outgrow the inheritance of uncaring viciousness. But being the current end-work of several billion years that have deposited in our brains and bones the genetic memory of witnessing or evading the brutal unkindness of nature, what has been recorded in the primitive part of our brain is inescapable. In witnessing an act of kindness, then, our entire evolutionary history tries to process this and is forced to conclude... this does not calculate. This does not figure. And the conflict between the sweetness of encountering good intentions and the visceral echos we carry of four billion years in which creatures only killed and ate one another cannot be easily or fully reconciled. A cognitive clash occurs, and so tears flow.

This is just one of many puzzles about being a long-surviving creature who, through millions of generations, has become more complex and learned to be amazed and to discuss and share ideas about this grand journey, this deep mystery. My paintings are my contribution to this investigation of our reality. I try to avoid the delusional and fantastical, just offer observations of the life we share with so many creatures and forces of nature.

Perhaps teaching our big brain somehow to not hear the ancient chatter of jungle and savannah will allow the small, recent voice of caring, which is certainly a part of our evolutionary success, to tell us something about where we are going. I don't know if my paintings can contribute to this kind of progress, but to observe and record, to sometime bemoan the pathos, sometimes laugh at the comedy, is an endlessly interesting project.

—Guy Colwell, 2025

LITTER BEACH

Oil on canvas • 1995–2002 • 87 × 96 in.
Ryan O'Connor Collection

Can you see the litter in this painting? Surprisingly, many people at first cannot. Our destruction of the planet is made worse by our unconsciousness. The ability to filter out the ugliness we perpetrate has been an historical and deplorable fact for as long as humans have been casting aside their waste. But, it may be changing. Remember when bottles, cans, plastic and paper blighted the streets of our city? I can remember the awfulness of it throughout the first half of my life. But better laws slowly emerged. Redemption of deposits and buy back and recycling of glass, plastic and metal have made a noticeable improvement on city streets. Yet, for many people who would never today drop a piece of refuse on the street, there is still little restraint in discarding items onto the natural world. I lived in an apartment in San Francisco adjoining a small piece of wild ground, with a couple of trees and some bushes. I was constantly amazed at how neighbors would come from blocks around — to drop every variety of garbage without thought on this one tiny patch of green.

Cast-off debris finds its way to the streams, to the seaside and to the ocean where vast islands of trash are still accreting and degrading the health of the planet. And since it is unseen by most of humanity, it is given little thought. Unconscious unseeing is the theme of this large painting.

Begun in 1995 as a kind of outdoor art-in-action project, I started painting it on the sidewalk of a busy and crowded part of town. But I could not sustain the burnout from doing such a monstrous undertaking it this environment. So I abandoned the work, and stored it in a friend's basement for several years. When I got to a more stable place, in a longer-term living situation with a real studio space, I recovered the big canvas and resumed work on it. So, in the end, it took seven years to complete, and became what may always be my Magnum Opus. Though, more than 80 years old now, I might still have time to outdo it.

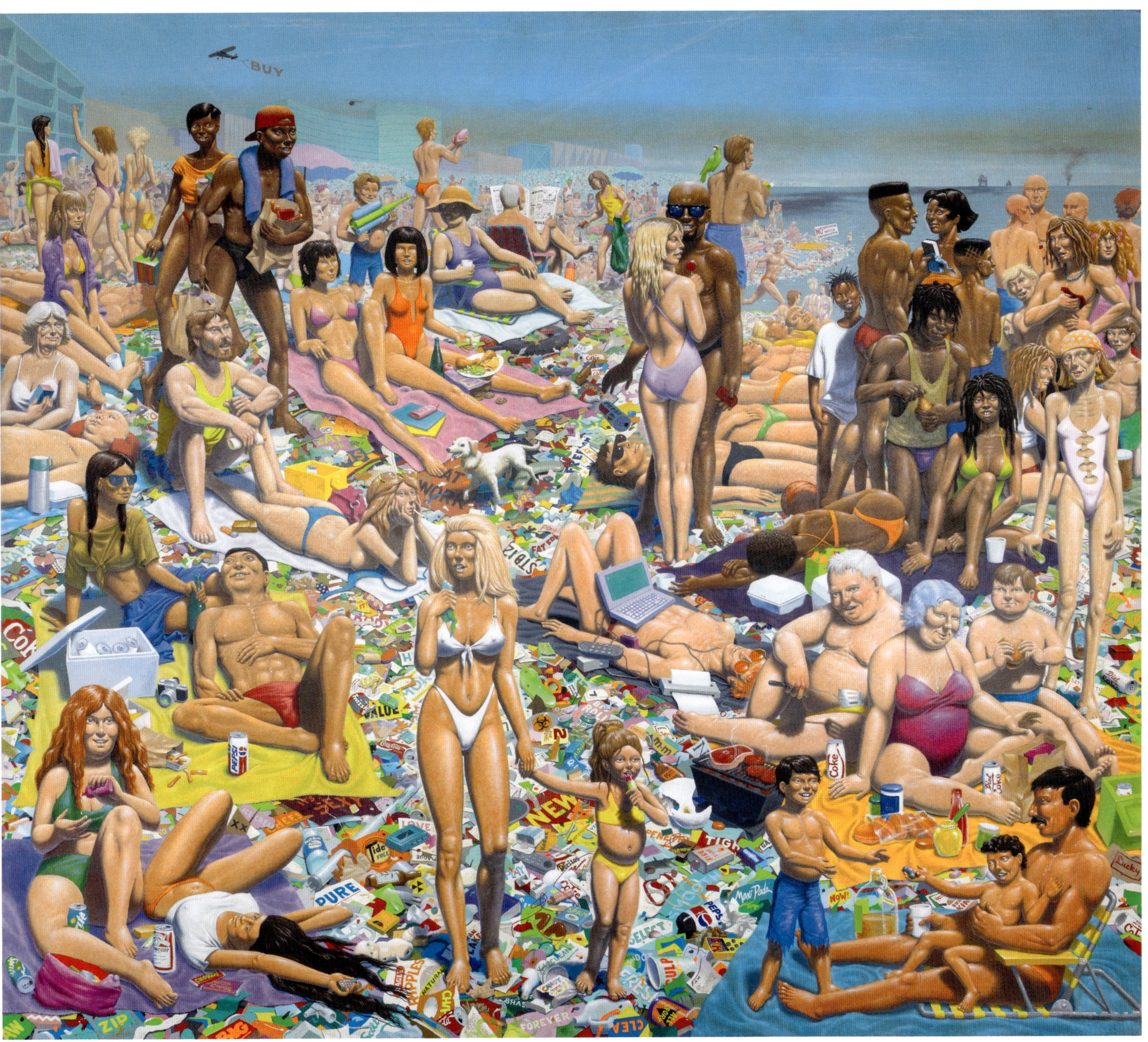
BUY
NEW
PURE
LOVE
FOREVER
Coke
PEPSI
Coke
Diet Coke
VALUE
ZIP

BREAD LINE

Acrylic on canvas • 2008 • 56 × 74 in.
Ryan O'Connor Collection

We may not always see the poverty around us, but it is there. Look for the food banks, the soup kitchens, the homeless shelters and the tent encampments. You can find clusters of desperate people. Unlike the affluent young woman with all her packages of shopping, passing by, unperturbed, and perhaps even unseeing, we should at least continue to be aware that the great wealth created by our system is not shared by everyone. So long as this gulf exists, the contrast between wealth and poverty should and will be an urgent subject for the visual artist to explore, just as it is for the sociologist, economist or political scientist.

Though I have lived through many years of struggle and at the edge of poverty, I've never been so hungry I've had to stand in line for a handout. I have also never possessed dazzling wealth. To me, having time to observe and record the conditions of life as I see them is the only real wealth. And it seems like the conditions I observe are in decline for more people. The original source of this picture was a food giveaway site in a poor part of the city that I would see on my way downtown. But since doing this painting, now there is another location doing handouts just one block from my house.

The only way I have actively helped to confront poverty and hunger has been, for a time, to participate in serving hot meals to very poor citizens, until the pandemic shut it down. But the contrast between wealth and poverty I put in this painting perhaps falls short of the reality. The one young woman with her abundance of packages should have been passing a line of many more — perhaps up to ninety-nine — hungry people.

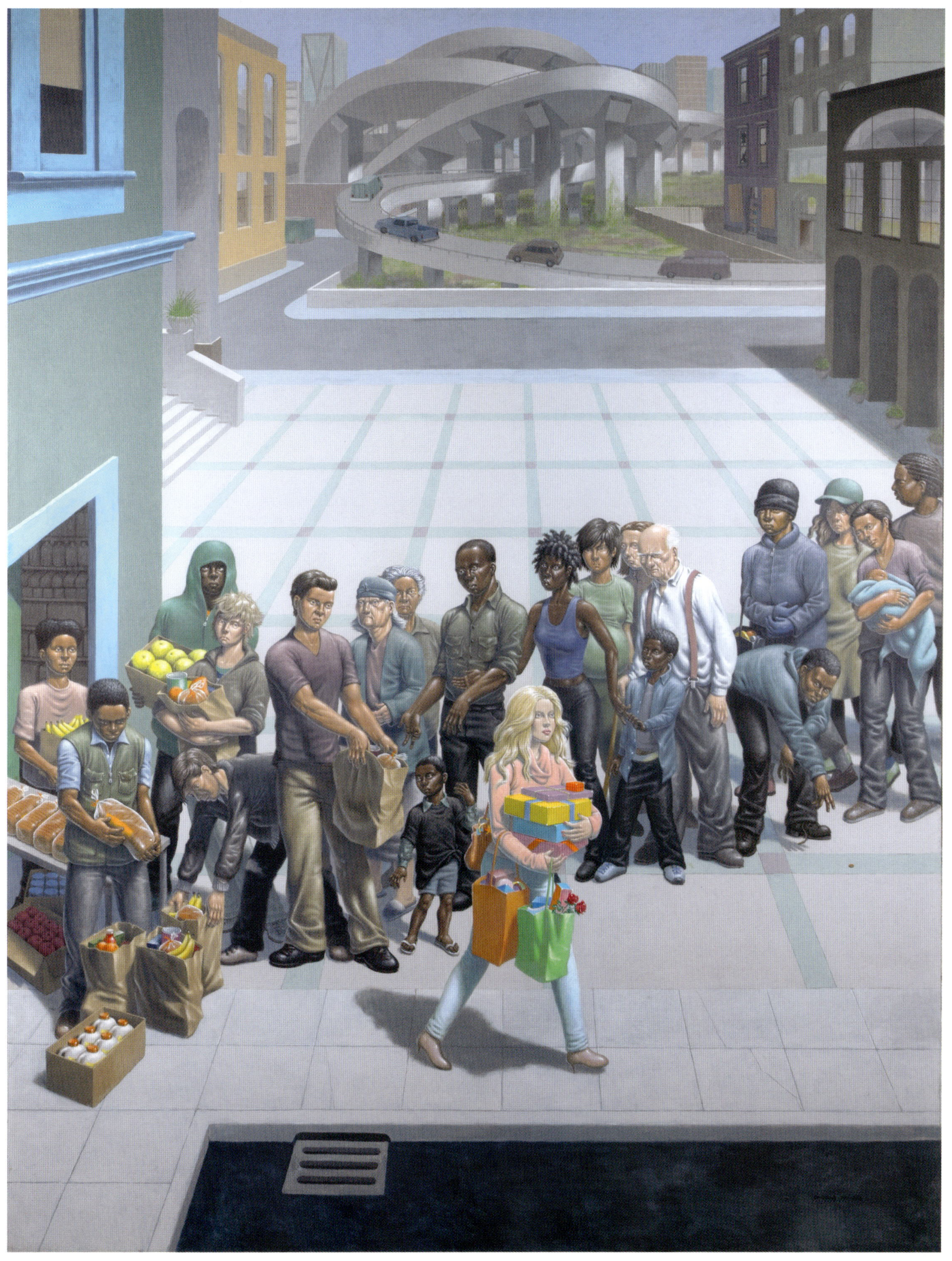

NOT EXACTLY PEACEABLE KINGDOM

Acrylic on canvas • 2012 • 52 × 66 in.
Ryan O'Connor Collection

We inhabit a small, crowded sphere. We have to live together with the many creatures that share this world, but we do not now nor have we ever lived in a peaceable paradise. The lion does not lie down with the lamb but rather tears it, dismembers it, consumes and digests it.

This is an inverted take on the famous paintings, numerous versions, by Edward Hicks. I suppose his images were inspired by a supposed biblical proposition that someway, somehow, hidden deep in the nature of things, there is an actual place and possibility where peace and harmony can exist with and within the natural world — probably dependent on the good behavior of our own species. I think we know better. Nature does not operate on the principle of kindness and compassion that we see fleetingly available between human beings. Even the nurturing we see in animal life is not an expression of caring but rather evolutionary programming that produces a slight reproductive and survival advantage for a species in a remorselessly cruel world. We can try to love them, protect them and preserve them, be awed by their beauty and power. But, in the end, they are not our friends and would as soon devour us as cuddle up to us.

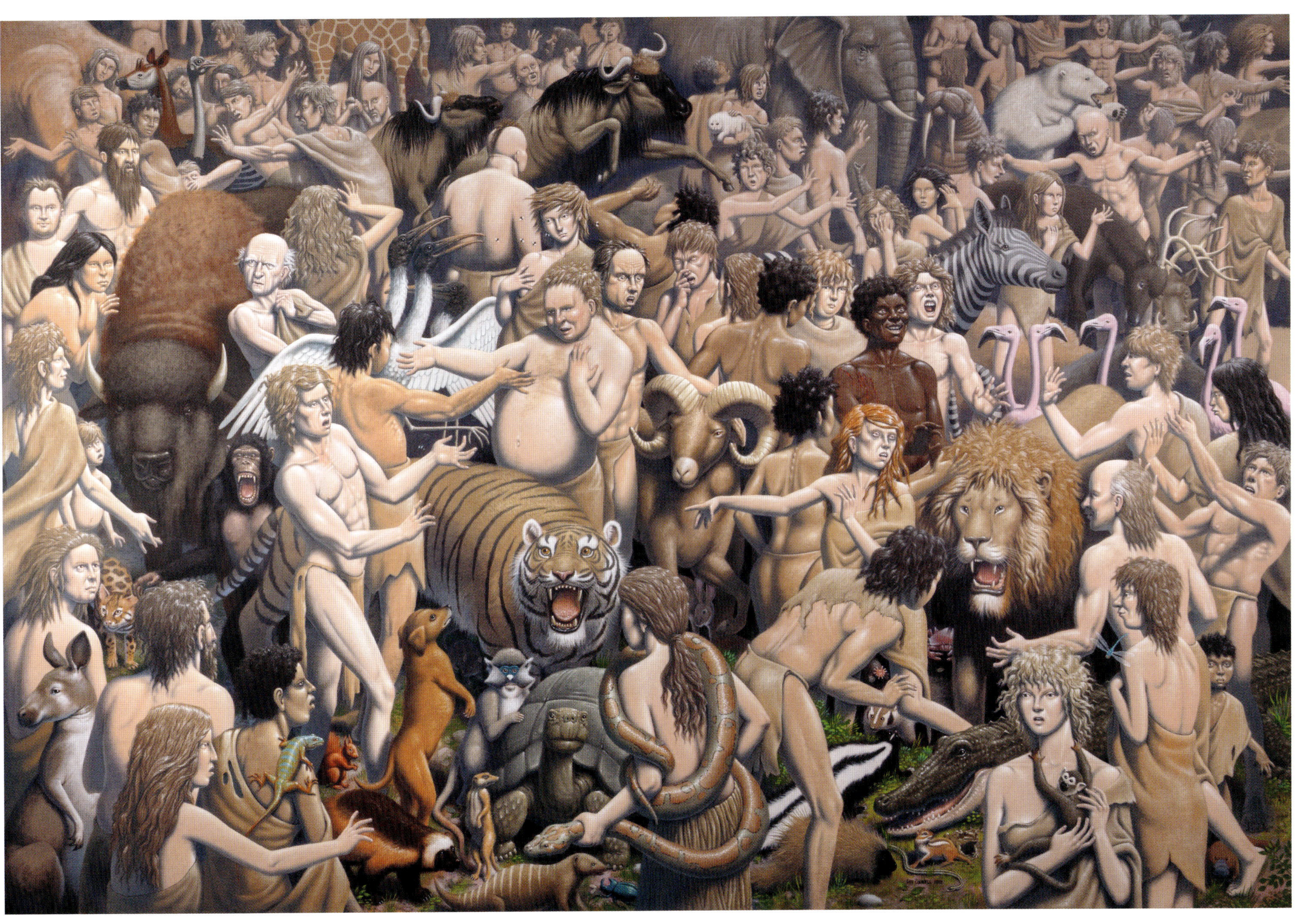

RECEPTION

Acrylic on canvas • 2008 • 30 × 39 in.
Private collection

This picture, contrasting rich/poor, work/fun, necessity/frivolity, has a personal and autobiographical slant. Its full title is *Reception: Self Portrait with Mop*. At the time I did this painting, I worked as a janitor for the Berkeley Repertory Theater, cleaning many spills and messes at many parties, openings and receptions. I used a style of crisp realism inspired by the work of Northern Renaissance masters like Van Eyck and Bruegel.

The fact is, other than painting pictures, I have nothing much in the way of marketable skills. Over and over, when I have tried to find employment, I start out looking for art jobs; graphic design, theatrical design, teaching, magazine illustration etc. I've had some success at this — comic book production at Rip Off Press, sculpture at Mattel Toys — but overall, my skills have been overlooked by paying employers, especially as I've gotten older. So, over and over, I've ended up in janitorial positions. I've learned a great deal about garbage and cleaning. So, this picture is a straight-ahead record of my work at the Berkeley Rep — mopping spilled wine at receptions, cleaning vomit and feces that somehow missed the toilet, struggling uselessly to reduce the population of drain flies, over and over and over — until I fell ill from exposure and exertion. Finally, I quit my last janitor gig at a Unitarian Church in 2019, just ahead of the pandemic. To make a visual reminiscence of my janitor years allowed me to approach the theme of economic inequality from a very personal place.

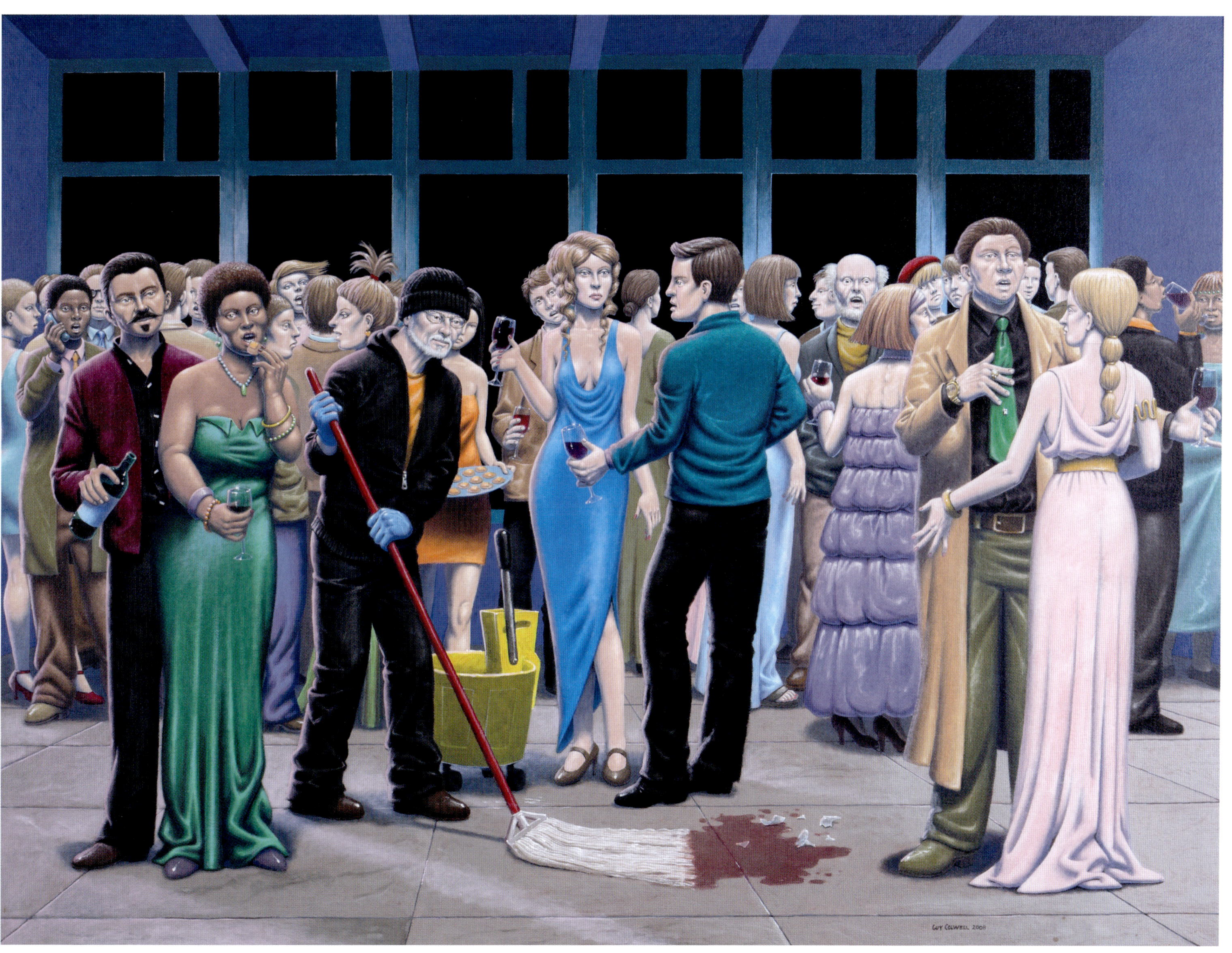

FOOD NOT BOMBS

Acrylic on canvas • 1994 • 45 × 55 in.
Owned by artist

Yes, why not feed the people instead of exploiting, oppressing or slaughtering them? A simple question. The message of this activist group, while it is being acted out on the local level, can be writ large on the international scene as well. We see so much hunger everywhere. There seems to be permanent drought and famine in Africa that we can do an even better job of alleviating. There is an abundance of food on this planet. It is only a matter of getting it to the people. Let's figure it out. Let's make sure everyone has enough. Why not?

I worked with the Berkeley Food Not Bombs group for a time in 1994. It was not so much as a social activist — not a long-term commitment — but a moment where my own activist tendencies intersected with an ongoing art project. It was one of those periods where I spent a good deal of time sketching people on the street, in coffeehouses, or at People's Park. It was there I was attracted to the Food Not Bombs Group when I saw the crowds of hungry street people gather for a bit of hot nourishment. As an extension of the live sketching I was doing, it became natural to fall in with them, join in the food prep and amass many sketches of the people and the process of feeding all comers. This painting was one of several that flowed from that period of activist art, and it fit well with the Social Realist focus of my work as a whole.

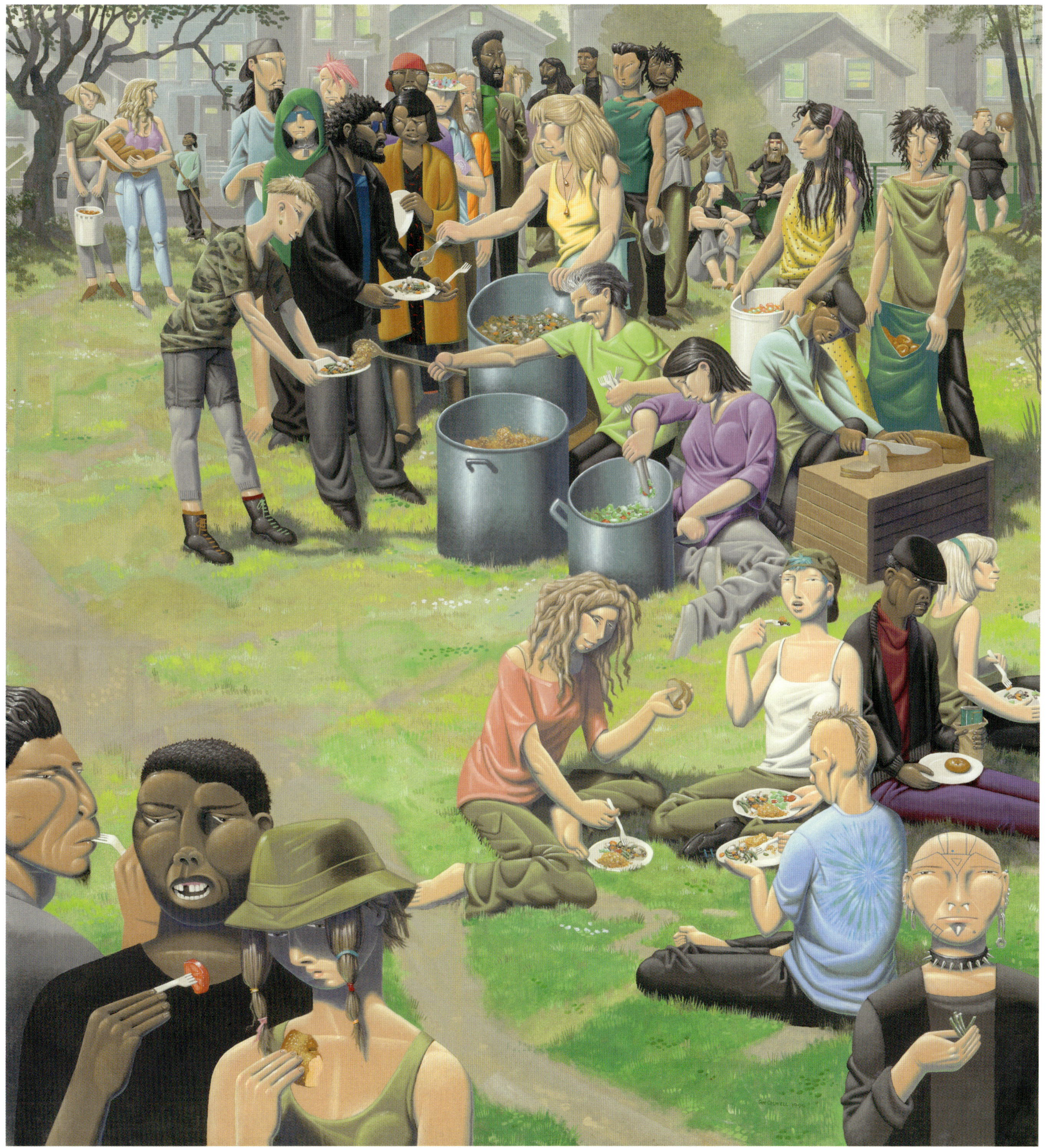

CANDY AND GUNS

Oil on canvas • 2006 • 36 × 45 in.
J. Paul Ghetto Collection

Got Guns? It is one thing to believe having a gun will offer security and protection in a dangerous world. It is quite another matter to give guns to children and recruit them into combat units. Not only can an easily manip-ulated child become a grotesquely fanatical killer playing soldier, but then the lives of so many young people have been effectively destroyed, childhood taken away, normal emotional and educational development brought to an end. Making revolution should be the work of serious and thoughtful adults, not children. And gun makers and dealers who exploit children in conflict situations for dirty profits should face harsh justice.

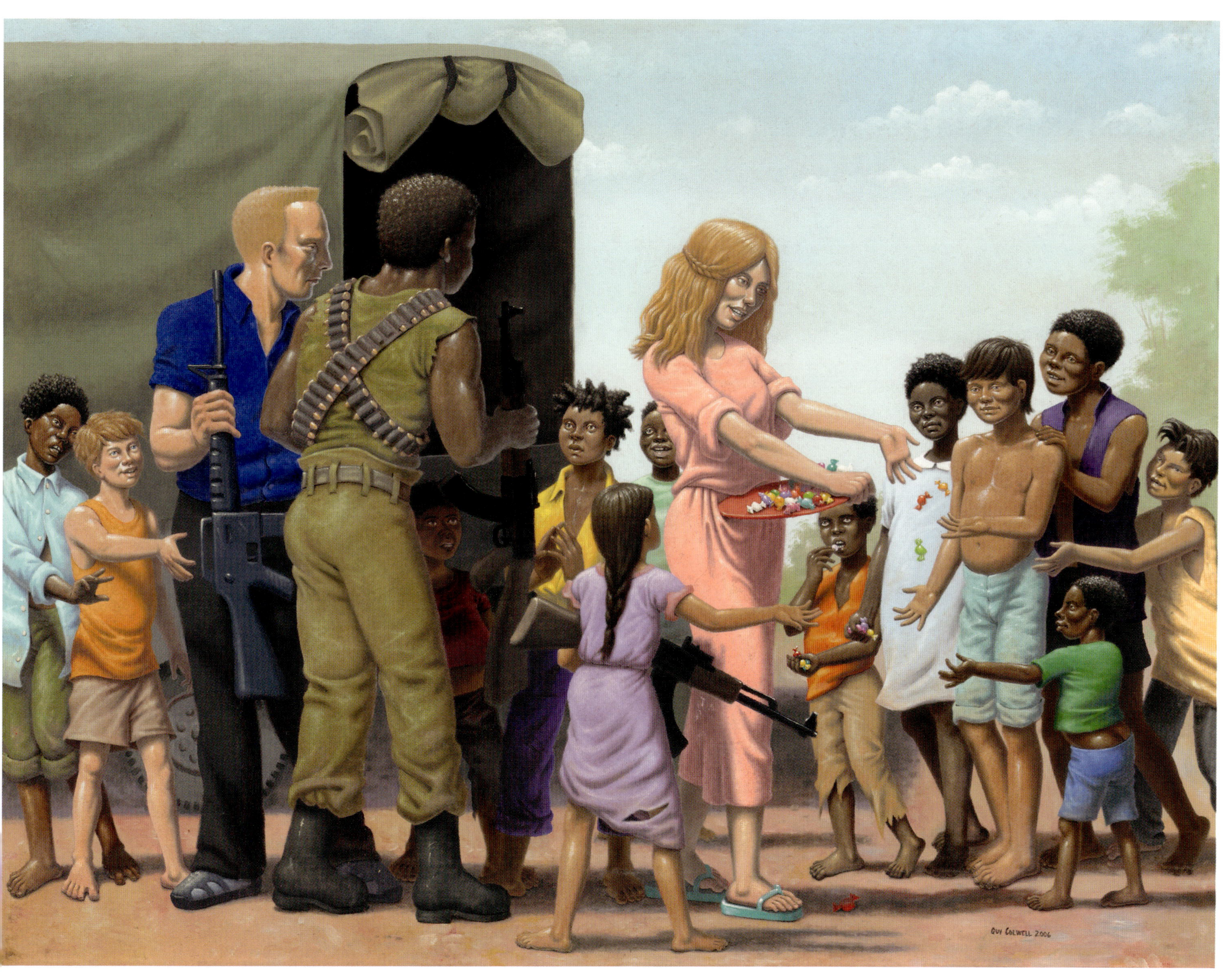

Qui Colwell 2006

DANCERS WANTING GRAVITY

Acrylic on canvas • 2010 • 39 × 55 in.
Ryan O'Connor Collection

It sometimes seems remarkable that, in a world still filled with violence, terror, hunger and destruction, many people, especially those from the richest countries, can dance and sing and party-on as if only happiness and pleasure exist. In the face of misery, violence and suffering, is this lack of gravity the best of all possible ways to point in the direction of happiness — or are stupidly frivolous people making things worse?

Just how serious do we have to be? Can't we dance wildly and celebrate ecstatically even while people are starving, being persecuted, slaughtered, bombed, burned and beaten down? There is an inappropriate level of disregard for the violence and suffering in the world by many who are living happy, well-fed lives and don't want the fun to stop. This painting began to take form in my mind after a so-called election in Iran triggered mass protests. The democratic and secular-inclined part of the population could not believe that the theocratic Islamists had so overwhelmingly won. What followed, as usual in authoritarian regimes, was the ferocious brutalization of the opposition. I hope we are not so busy being happy and partying that we fail to take seriously the repressive authoritarian Christo-Fascist bigotry that could emerge in the U.S. Then we won't be doing any joyous jumping around anymore.

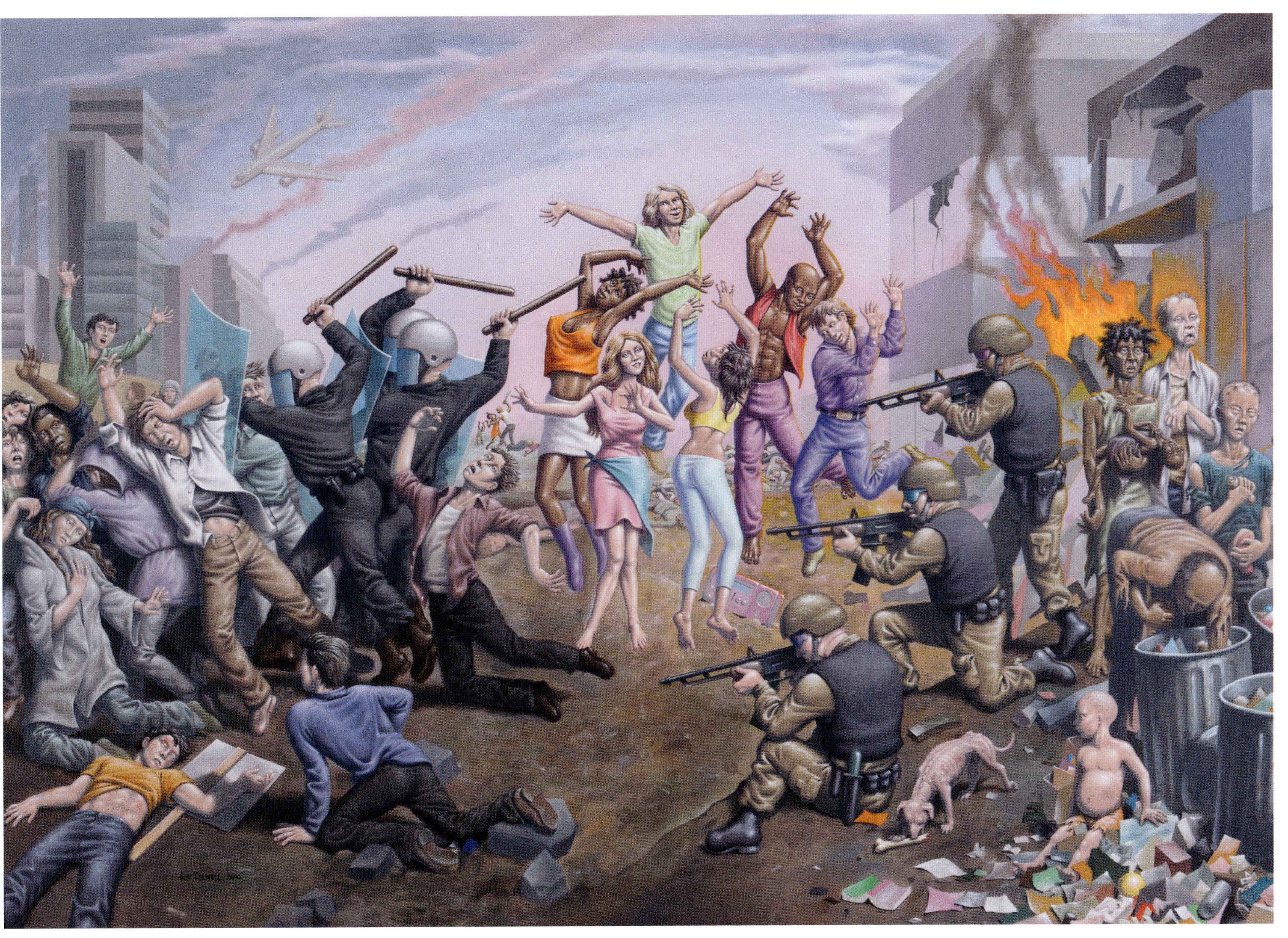
GUY COLWELL 2010

RECOVERING BODIES

Acrylic on canvas • 2006 • 37 × 48 in.
Owned by artist

Tragically, and all too often, scenes of bodies being recovered from devastated structures are not the result of natural disasters, but human violence. Whether it is events such as the Al Qaeda suicide attacks of 9/11, or the Israeli bombing of cities in Lebanon or Gaza, or the rocket attacks against Israeli cities or American bombing wherever in the world we have decided to intervene, these scenes come into our homes with painful frequency. We are compelled to ask these questions: Why do we do these things to one another? When will it stop? Can anyone ever be right when they are destroying cities and lives?

I happened to be in North Africa during an earlier Israel/Palestine conflict, several years prior to the Gaza War of 2024. Israel was bombing in response to Palestinian rocket attacks that had Israelis mostly living in shelters. The coverage I watched on Middle Eastern TV channels highlighted the destruction caused by Israeli bombs and showed especially numerous images of children being pulled from collapsed buildings. The coverage seemed more raw than the stories we see in the U.S. In some way, I had to record it, so I began a drawing that developed into this painting, which I executed upon returning to my studio. I can only call it a war protest — one that is especially dismaying as I watch the same scenarios play out again and again, year after year, with no solutions the belligerents are willing to embrace. Some paintings tied to a particular time or event become old news and of lesser interest after the event fades in memory. This one never seems to get old.

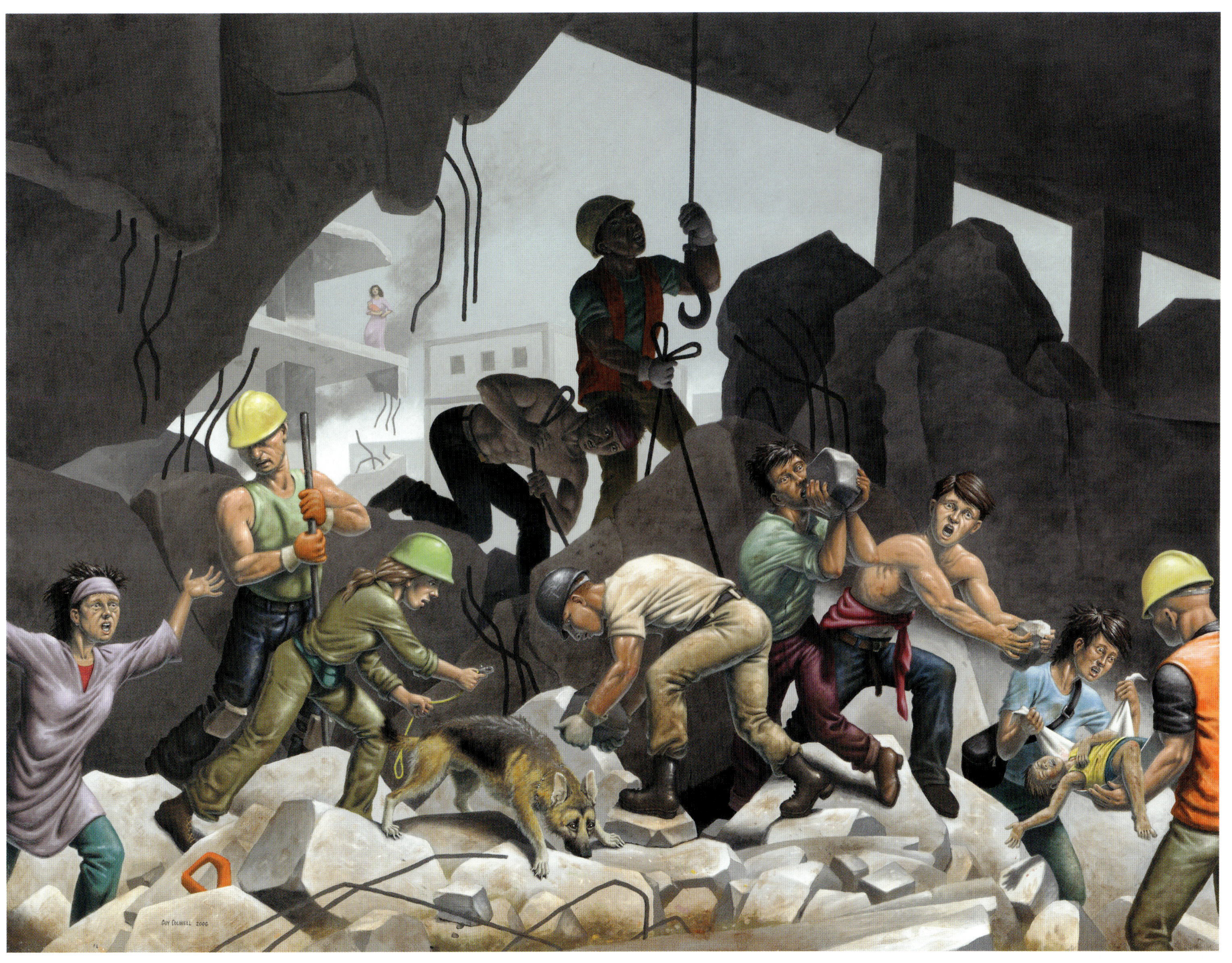
ROY COLWELL 2000

ANIMAL BOX

Oil on canvas • 2022 • 24 × 35 in.
Alex Seastrom Collection

A kind of younger sibling to the much-larger *Not Exactly Peaceable Kingdom*, this painting also explores the interconnected, possibly ambivalent relationship human beings have with the natural world. We share a small space, crowded together, interdependent. But we are the one species that holds all the rest in our care. It is an awesome responsibility. And we must care for them, not vanish them, not neglect them to death. This is because the world of living things depends on all life together making life possible for each living thing. Of course, this means if too many species die off more quickly than all the rest can adapt to a drastic shift, then a general and devastating collapse could occur. So, beautiful or awesome, gentle or ferocious, slimy or fuzzy: protecting and preserving any or all is how we preserve ourselves.

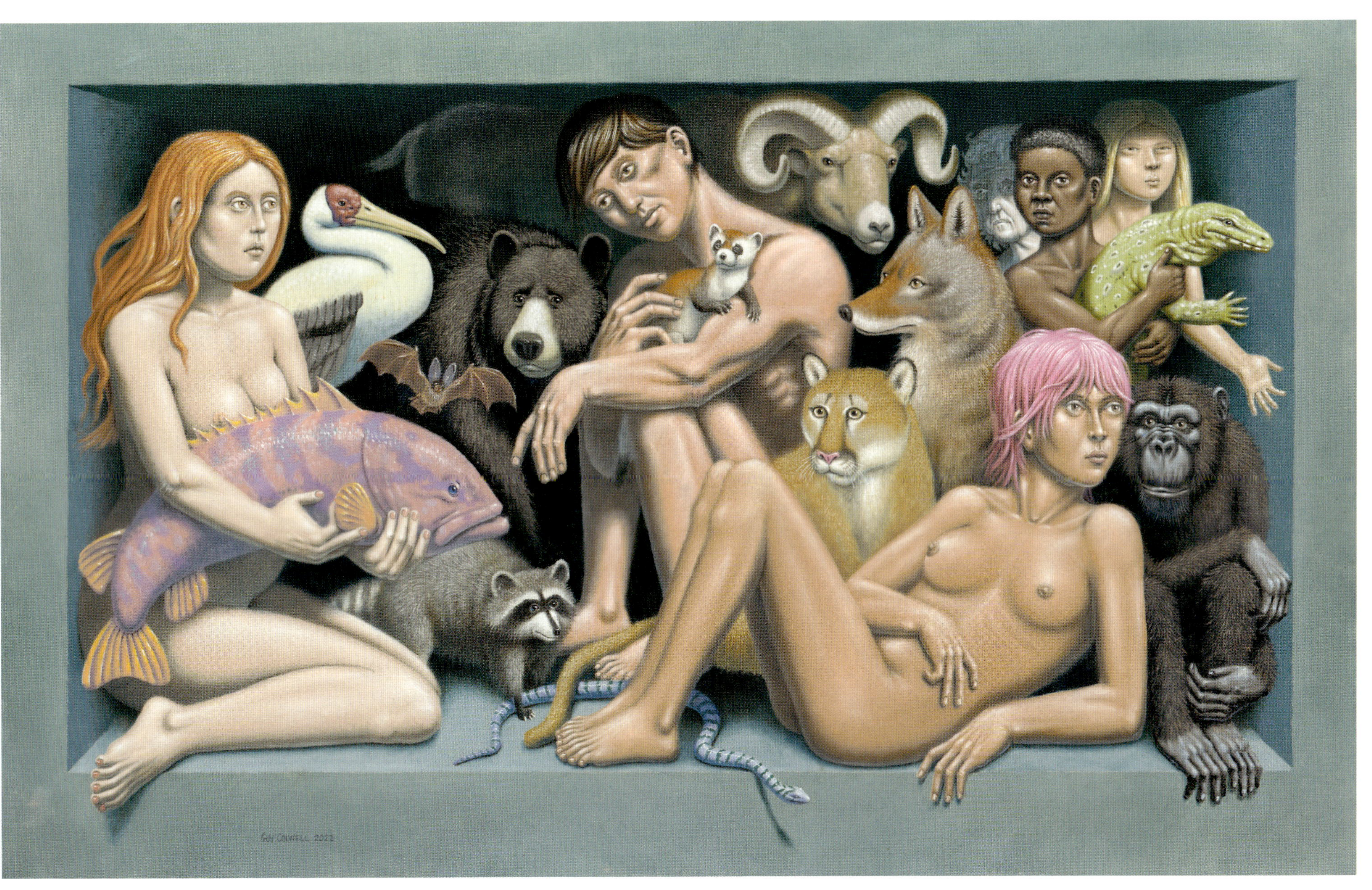

Guy Colwell 2022

SHIFT CHANGE, ICU

Oil on canvas • 2021 • 36 × 49 in.
Owned by artist

Pandemic brought the best out of some people. If not for the health-care professionals who put their own well-being in jeopardy every day — and many sacrificing their lives in the process — to help the sick stay alive, there would have been millions more fatalities from the virus. They are heroes and this painting honors them.

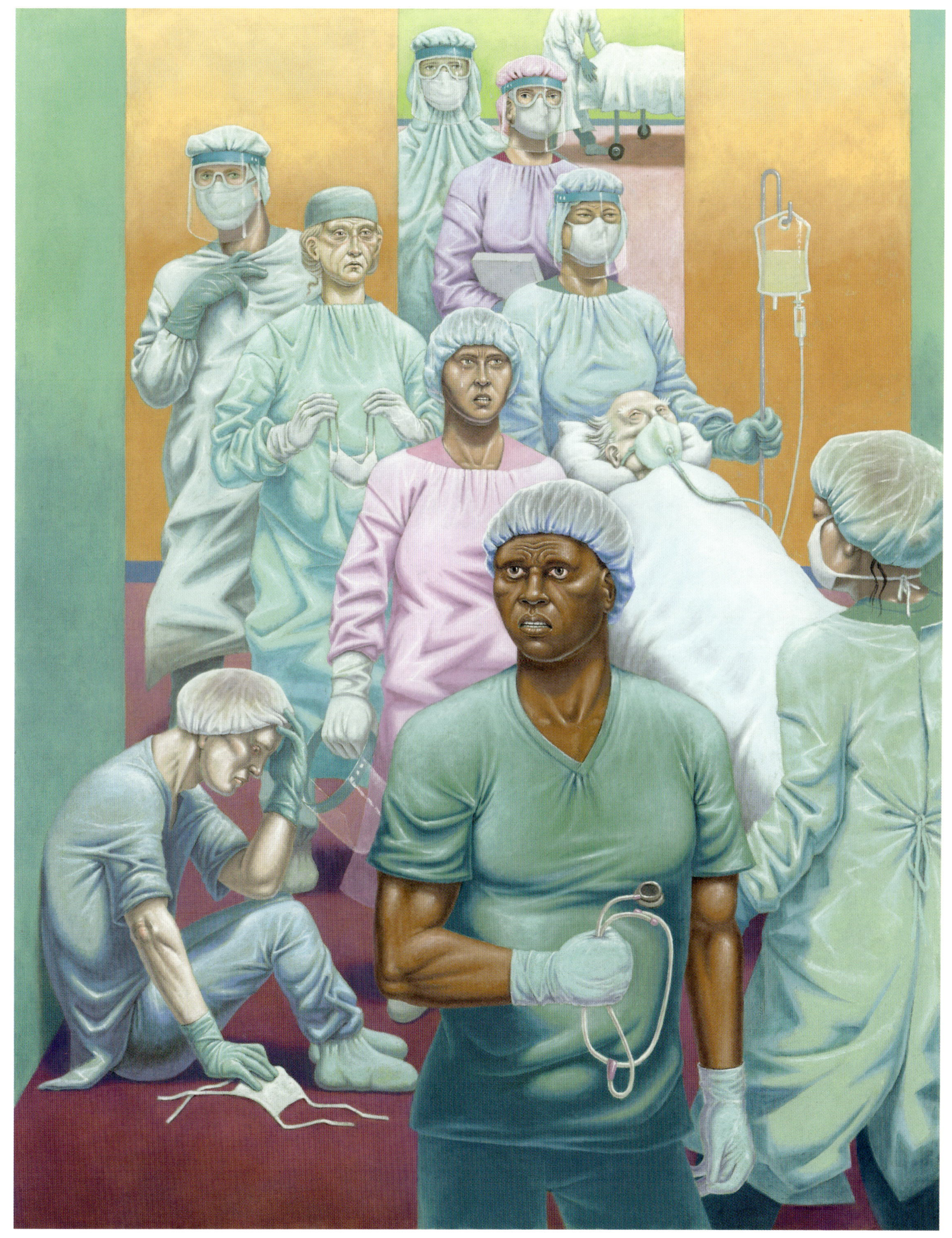

EBOLA TREATMENT CENTER

Oil on canvas • 2015 • 31 × 36 in.
J. Paul Ghetto Collection

The world has a right to be relieved when we hear that the recent African Ebola epidemics have been brought under control. It's scary, considering the ease with which any disease can travel wherever airplanes go, to think that our own hospitals looked like this in 1918 when the flu took down millions of people, and did again in the 2020s with the COVID-19 virus.

As I cogitated upon this painting and began a drawing for it, I couldn't help thinking of the late Medieval pictures of demons dragging the damned down to torment. And I thought, to be confined in an enclosed space, terrified, sick, bleeding out and surrounded by suffering, dying and dead people, must be a place more nearly like hell than any other we could experience.

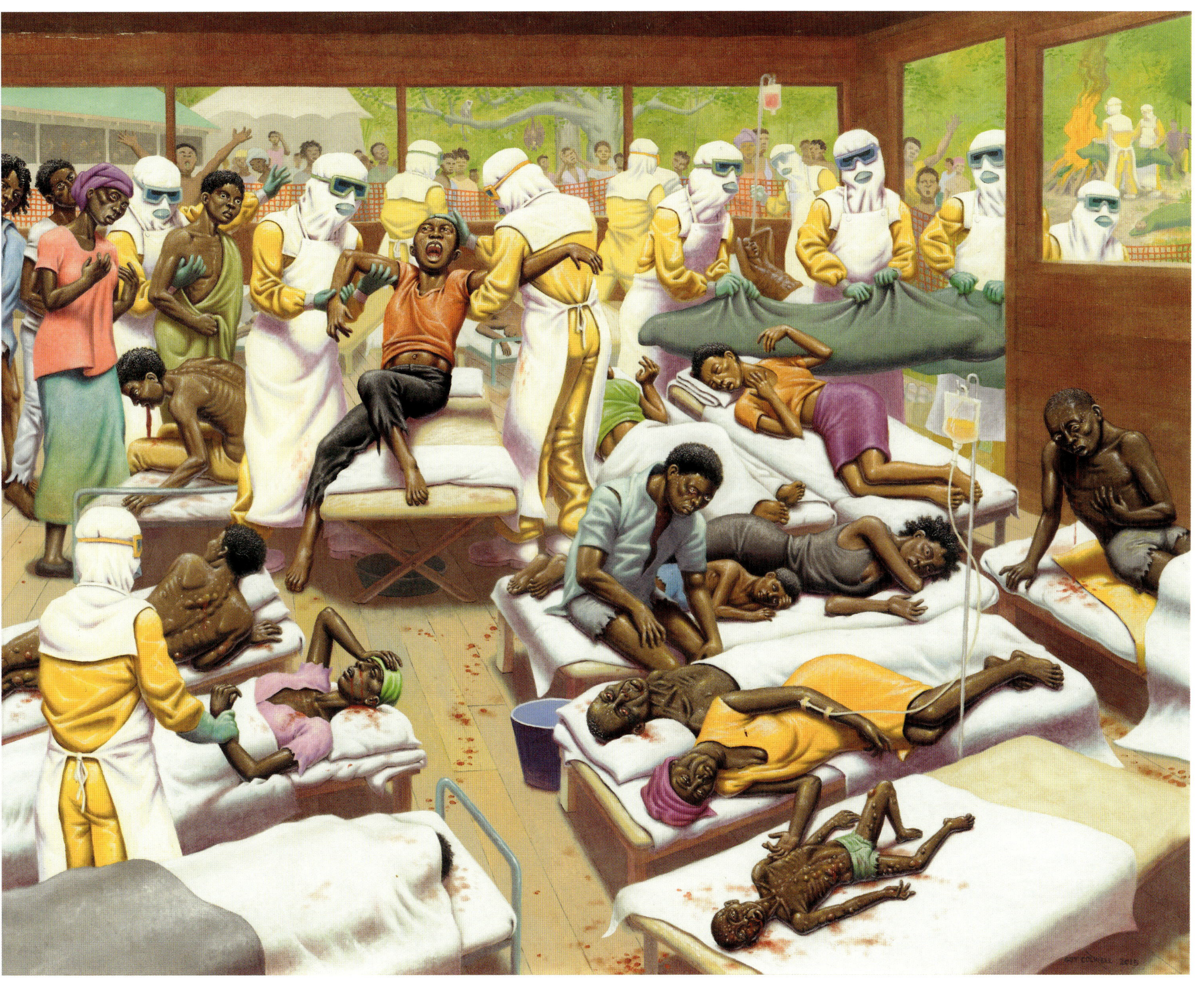

GANDHI'S MORNING

Oil on canvas • 1991 • 31 × 39 in.
J. Paul Ghetto Collection

Mohandas K. Gandhi was a complex man. Not only did he lead the Indian struggle for Independence, but he was a prolific journalist, a communal farmer and something of a physician with an emphasis on simple, natural remedies.

Gandhi was also a celibate. After fathering four children, he came to believe his own sexual behavior was unacceptably horrendous. His struggle with this part of himself came to a culminating crisis when his father died while he was copulating with his wife. He was so angered at himself that he renounced the sex act from that moment on.

But as Gandhi grew old and frail and unable to stay warm at night, he took up the practice of inviting one, or sometimes two, of his young female followers into his bed. I'm not clear if this was only for bodily warmth, or if he wished to continually test the strength of his resolve to be abstinent. Or perhaps it was just sex by a different, noncoital means.

This painting imagines a quiet morning in the ashram with Gandhi administering one of his simple medical remedies, an enema, to a young but constipated follower.

It's all true. Read a bio of the Bapu.

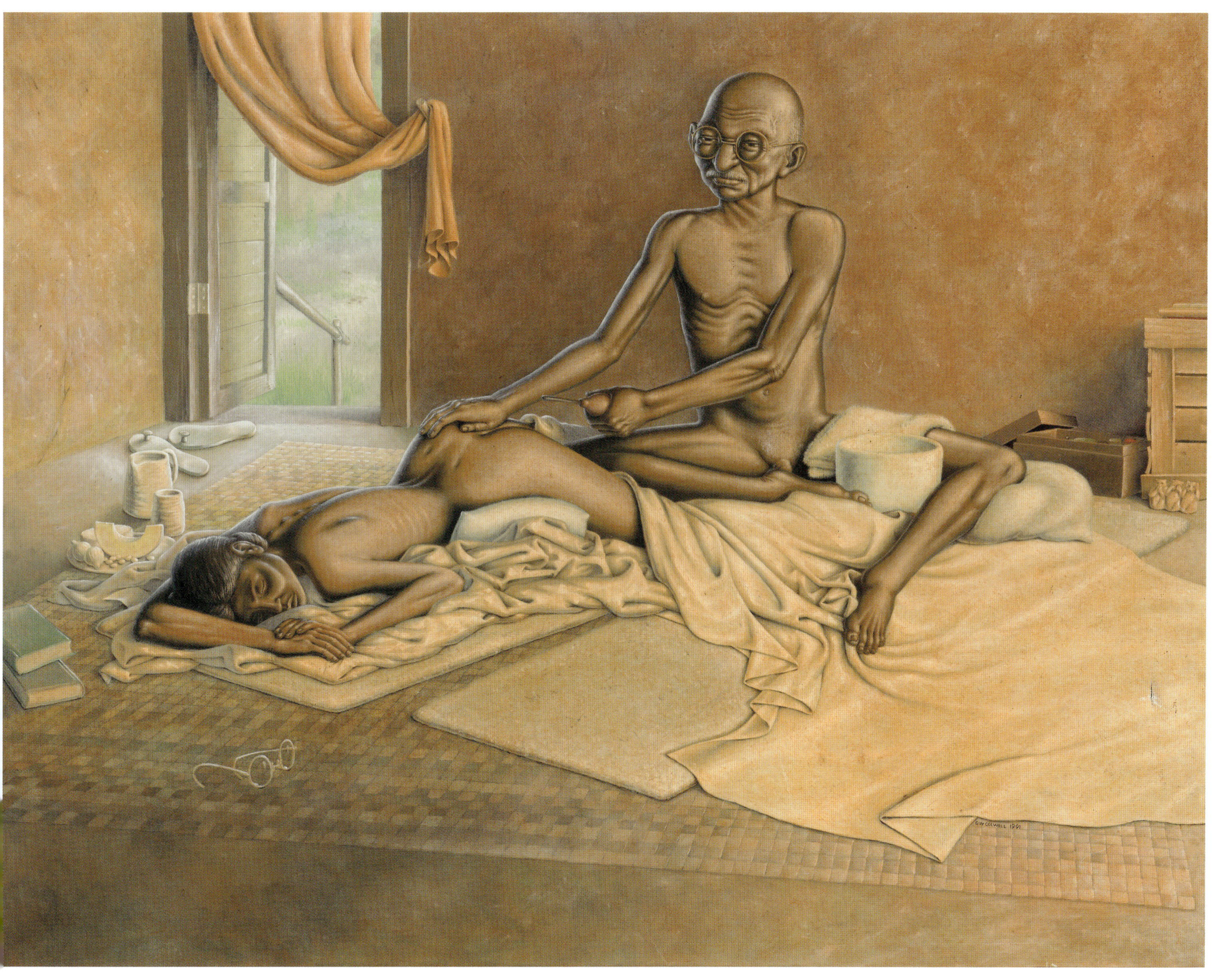

EPIDEMIC

Acrylic on canvas • 2009 • 34 × 50 in.
Crocker Art Museum, Sacramento

COVID-19 won't be the last Epidemic, and probably not the worst. The way Natural Selection works and the patterns of human activity make it inevitable. The viruses and bacteria best able to evade immune systems and medical interventions will multiply and spread. Jet planes will carry the improved superbugs around the planet. As we devise ways to beat down one wave of sickness, others will be rolling toward us in an unending queue of pathogens.

This painting from 2009 reflects on an earlier wave of sickness as it radiated around the world. That time, it was an H1N1 flu. Though not as deadly as COVID-19, burning itself out quickly, it still raised great alarm for a few weeks.

Study the faces in this painting and you can see who is sick and who is not yet sick as the virus marches across the canvas.

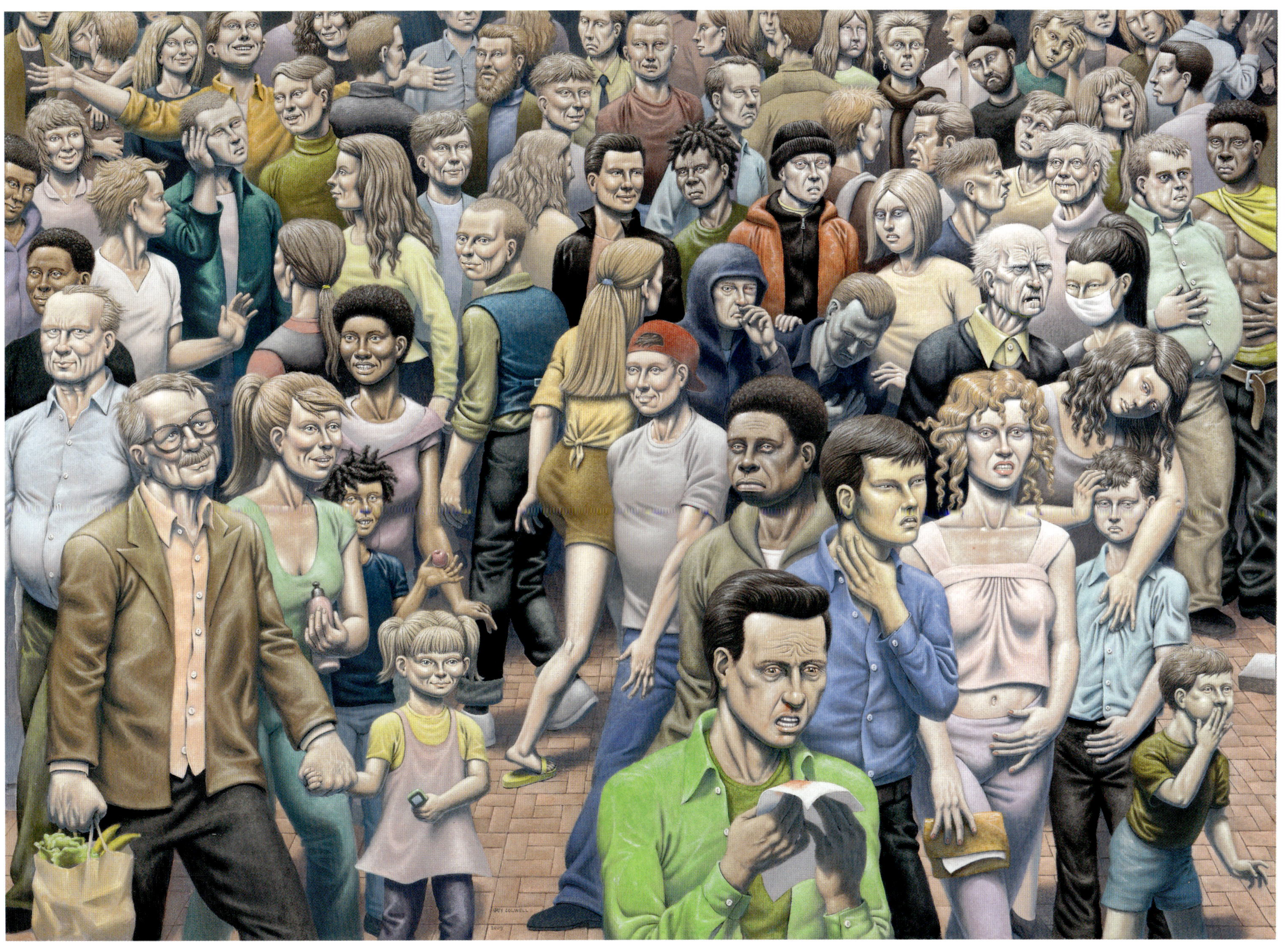

X-PLICIT PLAYERS

Acrylic on canvas • 1994 • 27 × 42 in.
Owned by artist

This painting is more journalistic than surrealistic. I got to know the group, calling themselves the X-Plicit Players, back in 1994. They would appear, from time to time, on Berkeley's Telegraph Avenue, and do a slow, rhythmic dance while playing their didgeridoos, always totally nude. They also organized indoor events in clubs or in their communal house, where groups of people would put aside their clothing and do a kind of ritualized, though quite controlled, set of exercises. These, I suppose, were intended to teach how to feel comfortable and self-accepting in a state of raw vulnerability. Because they knew I was working on a painting about them, I was invited to a couple of the events. I found them interesting but not transforming. It seemed, in a world full of poverty, war, hunger, inequality, climate crisis, conflict, crime and uncertainty about the prospects for the planet to survive and thrive, perhaps a bit on the inconsequential side.

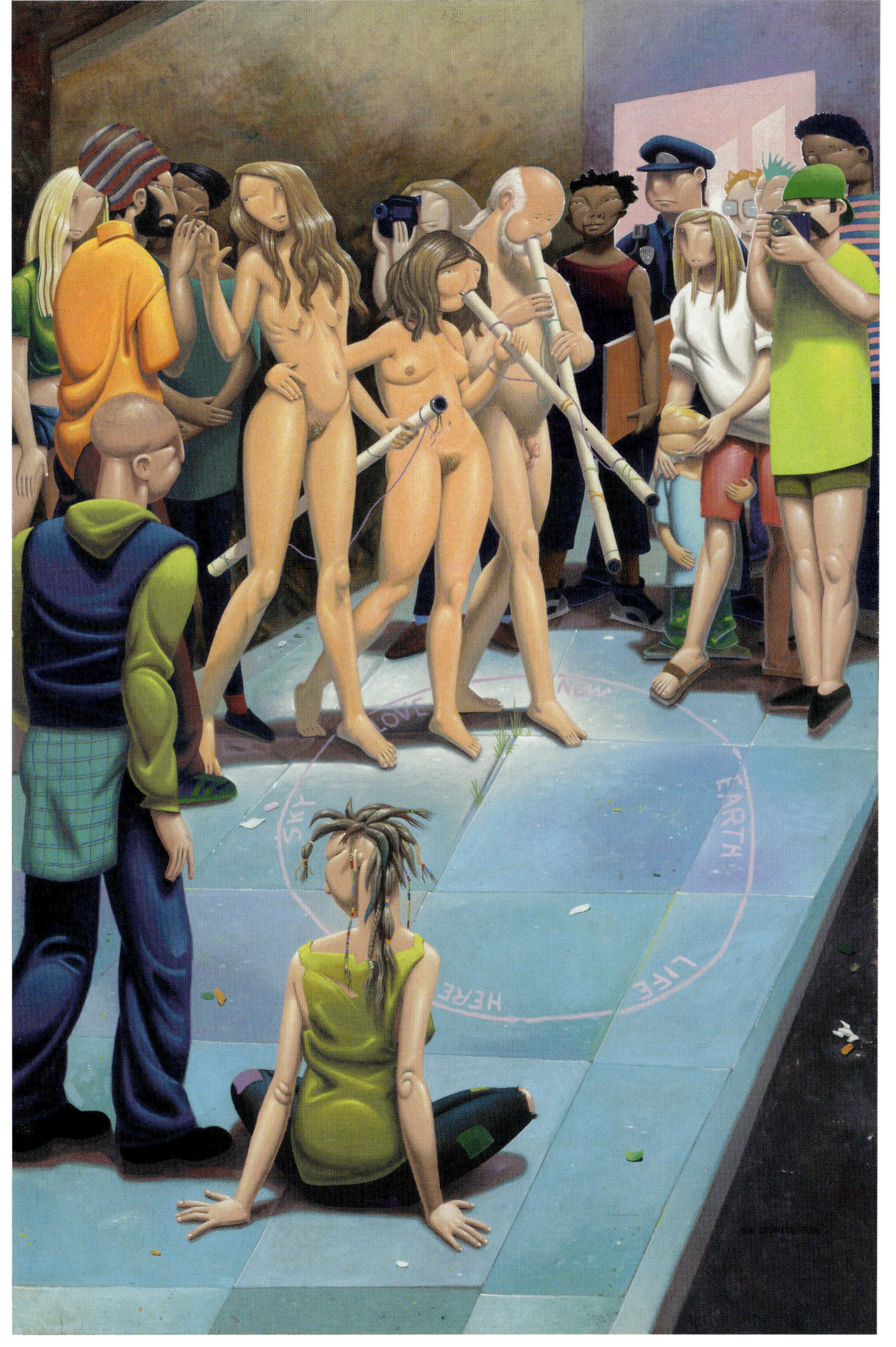

SKY
LOVE
NOW
EARTH
LIFE
HERE

BOOTY DAY

Oil on canvas • 2023 • 28 × 43 in.
Alex Seastrom Collection

Male gaze, Female display. These powerful urges, sometimes deeply repressed, sometimes just under the surface, sometimes full blast in public places, are part of us. They may annoy, frighten, offend, shock, tempt, torment or harass us, but hidden or overt, they are some of the deep evolutionary programming that make us the human animals we are. It's really all a consequence natural selection has devised to bring sperm and egg together so we will go on, like all life, making more males and females who will make more males and females who will make… and so on.

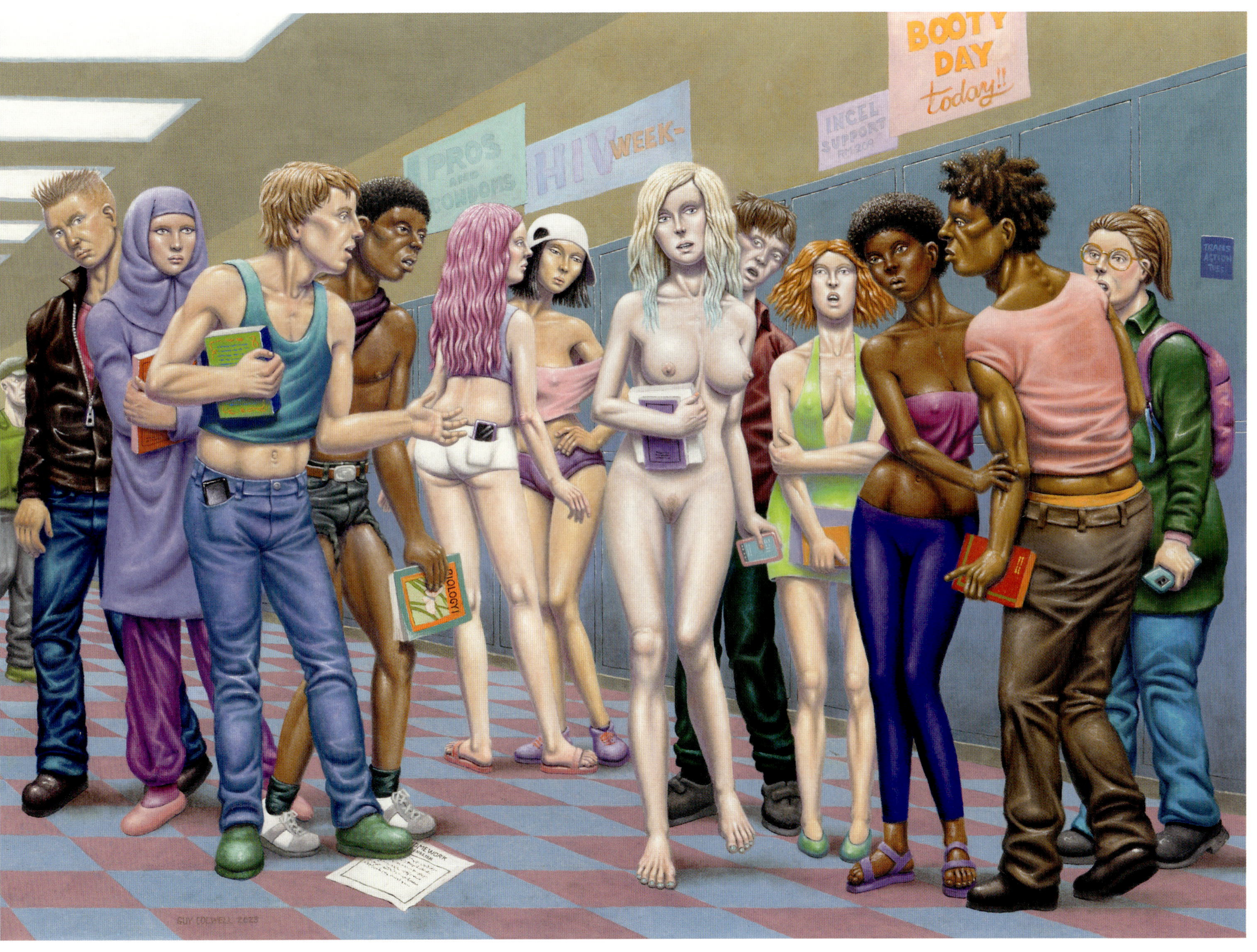

PROS AND CONDOMS
HIV WEEK-
BOOTY DAY today!!
INCEL SUPPORT RM 309
TRANS ACTION TI.5
BIOLOGY

HISSING

Oil on canvas • 1991 • 16 × 30 in.
Owned by artist

Men posture and strut, flex their muscles and try to act dangerous to maintain a sense of their manhood. But the sight of an attractive young woman can deflate the strongest of men into blustering, stammering and sputtering discombobulation. A pretty face and nubile body will make a man feel weak, even helpless, when gripped by biological forces so powerful they can reduce a strong man to expressions that come wordless from deep primal spaces. And the beast may despise beauty for so effortlessly undoing the pretense of manly strength, with anger and hatred flowing on a surge of lust.

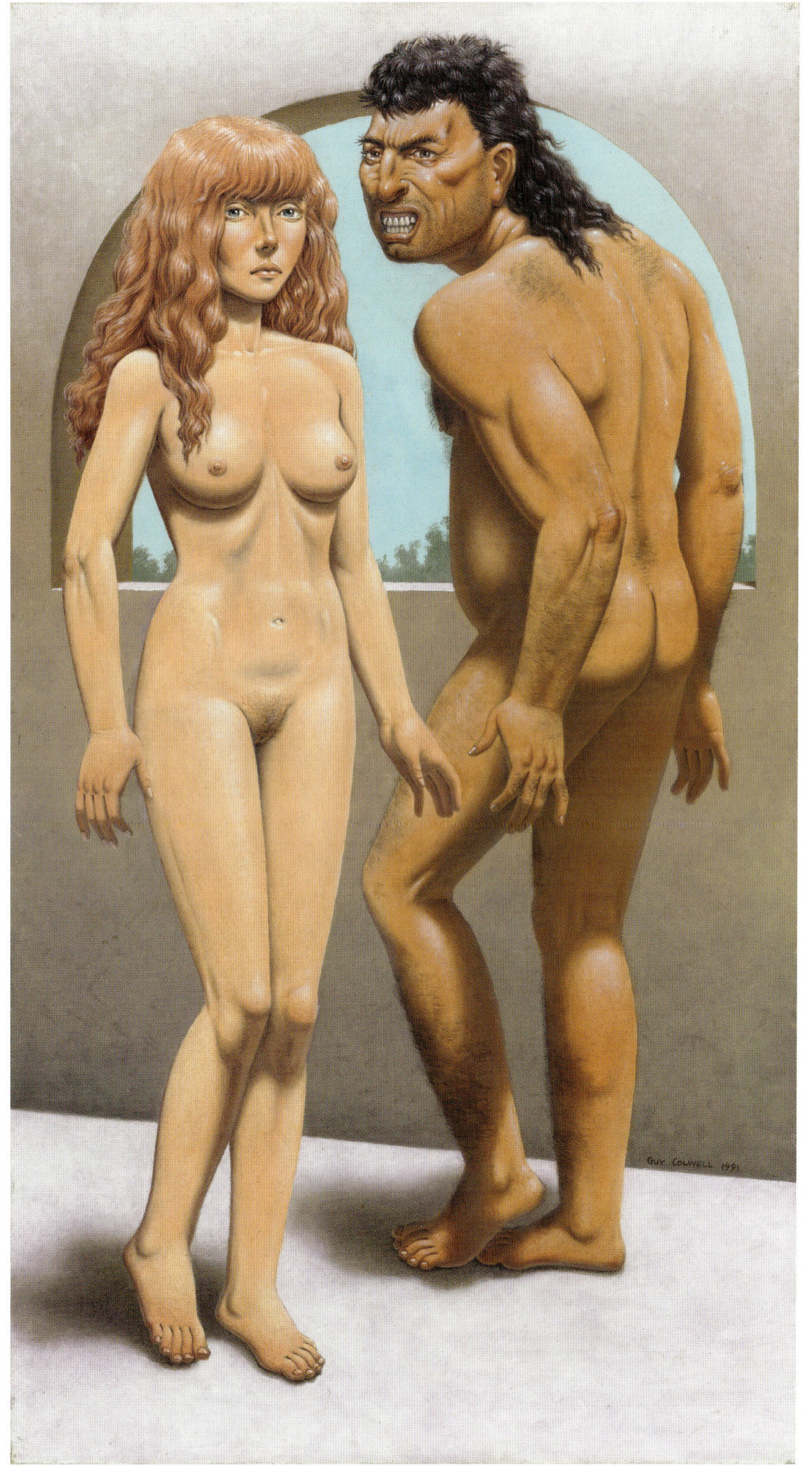

ROCKPILE

Acrylic on canvas • 1992 • 28 × 34 in.
Private collection

When I was living in a motor home in Auburn, California, and working for Rip Off Press doing comic book production, I organized life-drawing workshops at the Auburn Art Center. It was there I did the sketch that would be the basis of the figure in this painting.

In Auburn, I would often take my home-on-wheels higher into the Sierras to have some wild nature and sketching time. One one weekend, I was out on the Yuba River hiking with my sketchbook, and I passed numerous towers of rock, some quite unbelievably tall and entrancing. So I sketched one of them.

I put the woman and this rock pile together for a picture that was quickly snatched up by a collector and disappeared, except for a good photo transparency that was used for this book. It is one of those pictures I really miss because it reminded me of a special, calmer, simpler time, closer to mountains and rocks and trees and water. Probably because times like that are so fleeting, I had to include a symbol of impermanence in the form a skull lurking in the water.

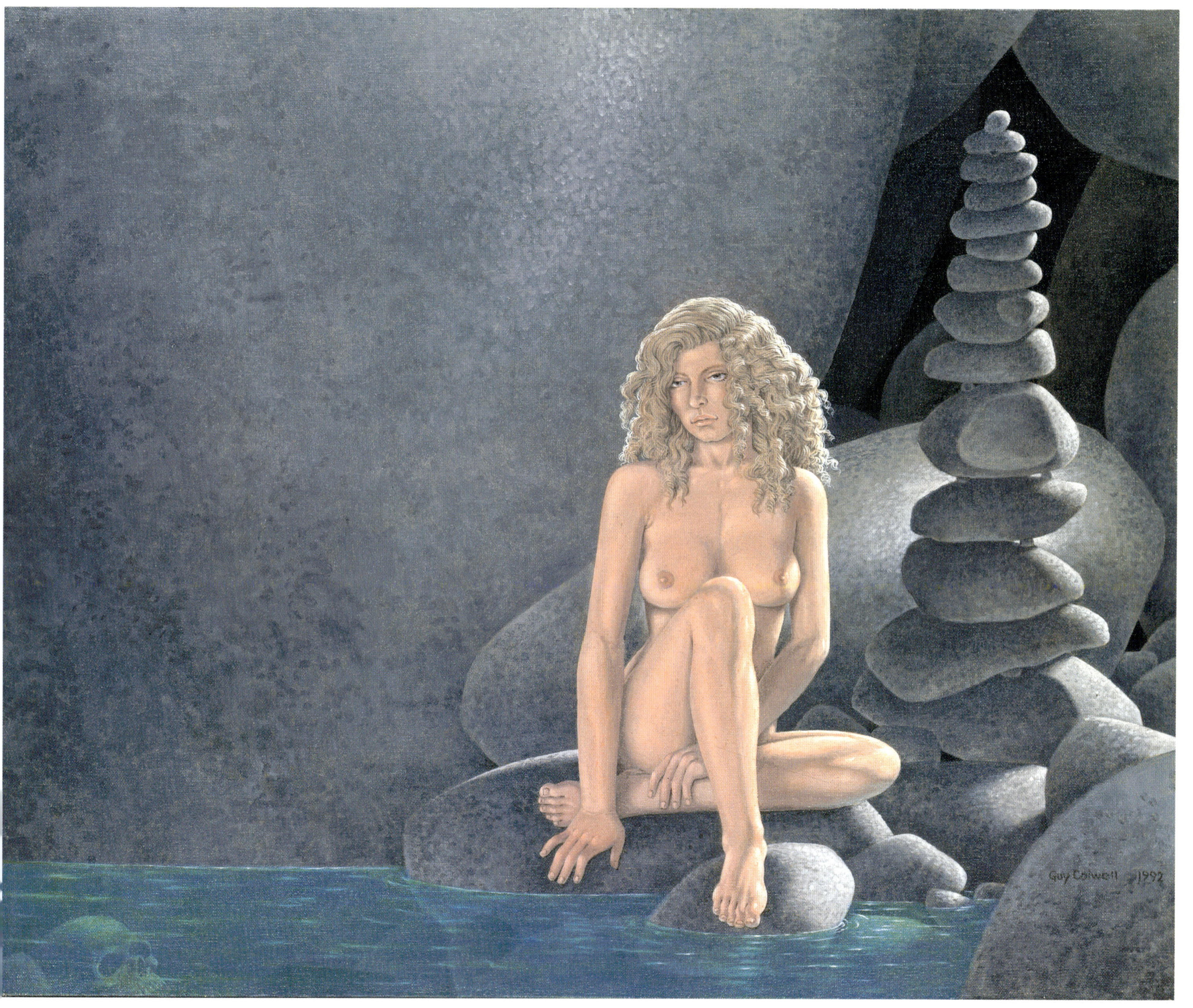

Guy Colwell 1992

LITTLE THEATER

Acrylic on canvas • 2005 • 28 × 32 in.
Owned by artist

There is always a piece of natural animal reality lurking in our mind-space. It's in us and can be expected to take the stage at any moment to remind us who we are and where we came from, what made us, follows us — it will not stop being a part of us.

In this picture, I believe I am reminiscing nostalgically about the several times I have made tentative approaches to the field of Theatrical Design. I have tried creating sets numerous times. Mostly, these have been done almost as a hobby to keep my hand in an activity that pulled at me strongly going back to my high school days. Only once did I design and build a set that was actually used. This was for a small community theater production of *A Midsummer Night's Dream*. Other than this, I've only built scale model sets as examples to show to theater companies, or I put stage sets into paintings as I did in this piece. But, alas, my only actual paid theater work was as a janitor for the Berkeley Repertory Theater, where I submitted some of my models — but they couldn't get their minds around the possibility a janitor might have skills and interests in this direction.

I also brought a little piece of Africa into this picture by using a sketch I did close up of a Sable antelope confined in an enclosure in Zambia for some reason I never found out.

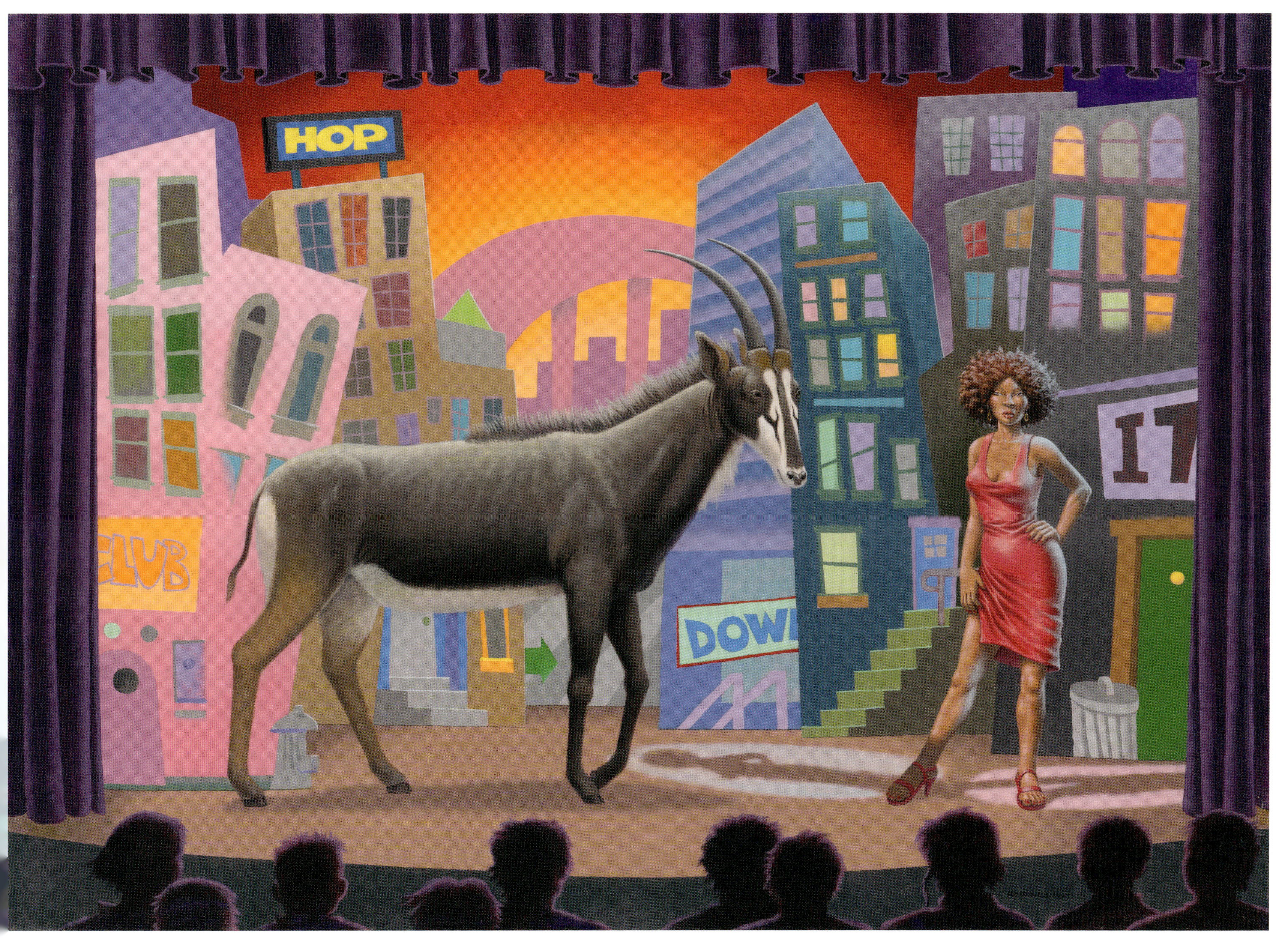
HOP
CLUB
DOW
IT

PAINTER WITH GENET

Acrylic on canvas • 2005 • 26 × 30 in.
Ryan O'Connor Collection

A painter lets out his expressionistic animal: a creative process as unpredictable and startling as an unexpected encounter with an exotic beast. The artistic outcome, relying more on the laws of motion and gravity than any kind of technical skill, might actually be intriguing for art lovers to see. But the temptation to think, "I could do that just as well myself," will probably enter their minds.

Like movies about Hollywood, I have done numerous paintings about painting, or about painters or about showing paintings. They have titles like *Little Gallery*, *Abstract with Female Element*, *The Celebrated Painter*, *Expressionist Pausing*, *Painting Inside My RV*, *Demon Painter*, *Woman Meets Rhino in an Art Museum*, and others. Of course, in some sense, every painting is about painting. We have to constantly explore the act and the meaning of this occupation, or perhaps, this obsessive compulsion. We have to practice, study, experiment, take risks and dig deeper and deeper into the mystery of why we need to spread pigments on surfaces until we get to the end place, where it is done completely right, which is to say, there is never an end to it.

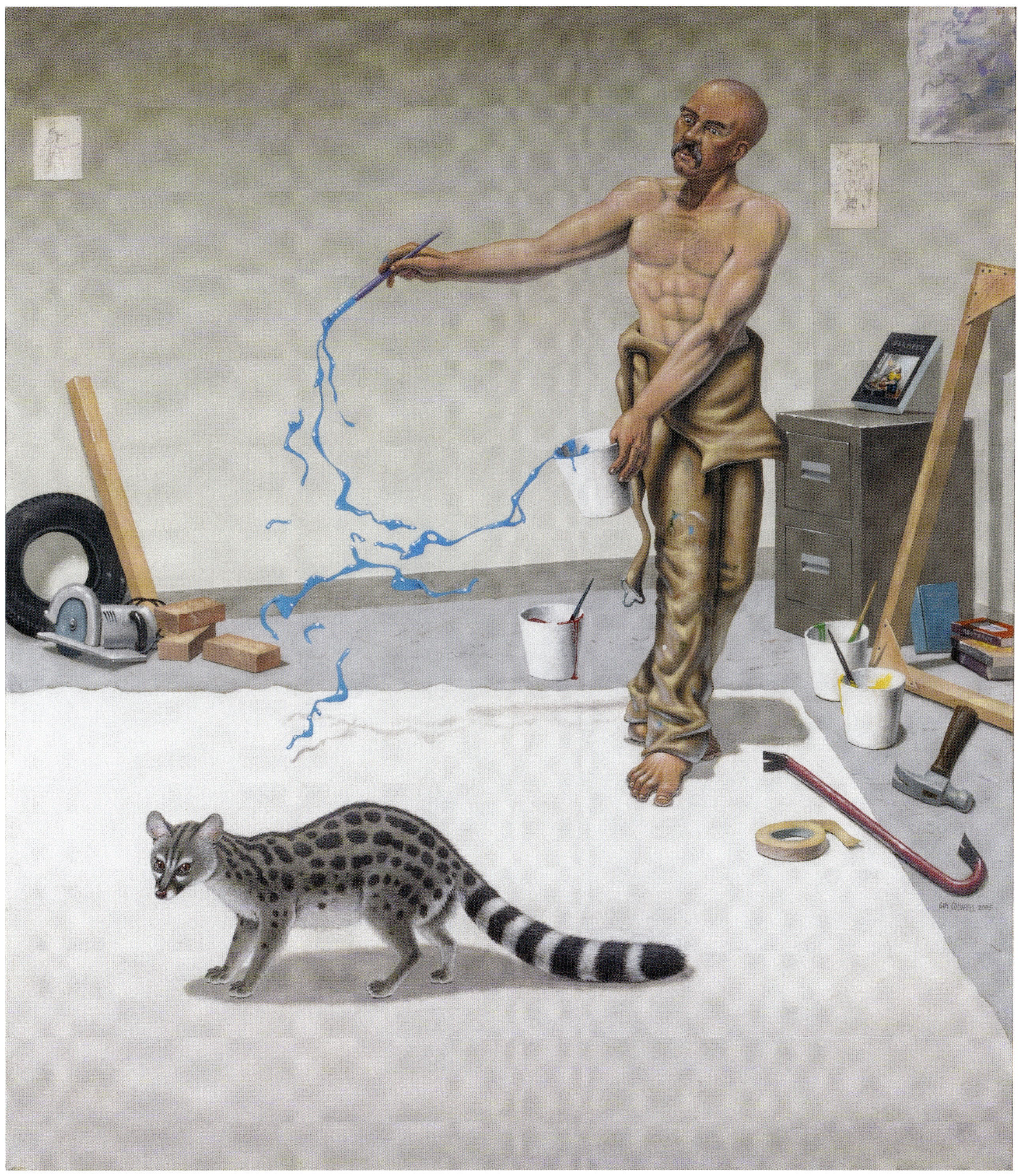

GRAVE MAN WITH KITTEN

Oil on panel • 2016 • 13 × 15 in.
Owned by artist

A study in contrasts. The man, grave, angry and maybe a little dangerous, is incongruously stroking a soft, furry kitten. There is a small jolt of surprise here: to see this unexpected juxtaposition and a suggestion that every person has complexities and layers not visible on the surface. I'm not sure I can say now exactly where this picture came from. My mom, I know, loved white cats and I watched many white kittens being born. Maybe I just wanted to do a bump of cool blue light. Maybe I was intrigued to paint an angry face, or a bare chest or a kitten. I can't remember how it started, but I like it a lot, and it has managed to get shown in numerous galleries.

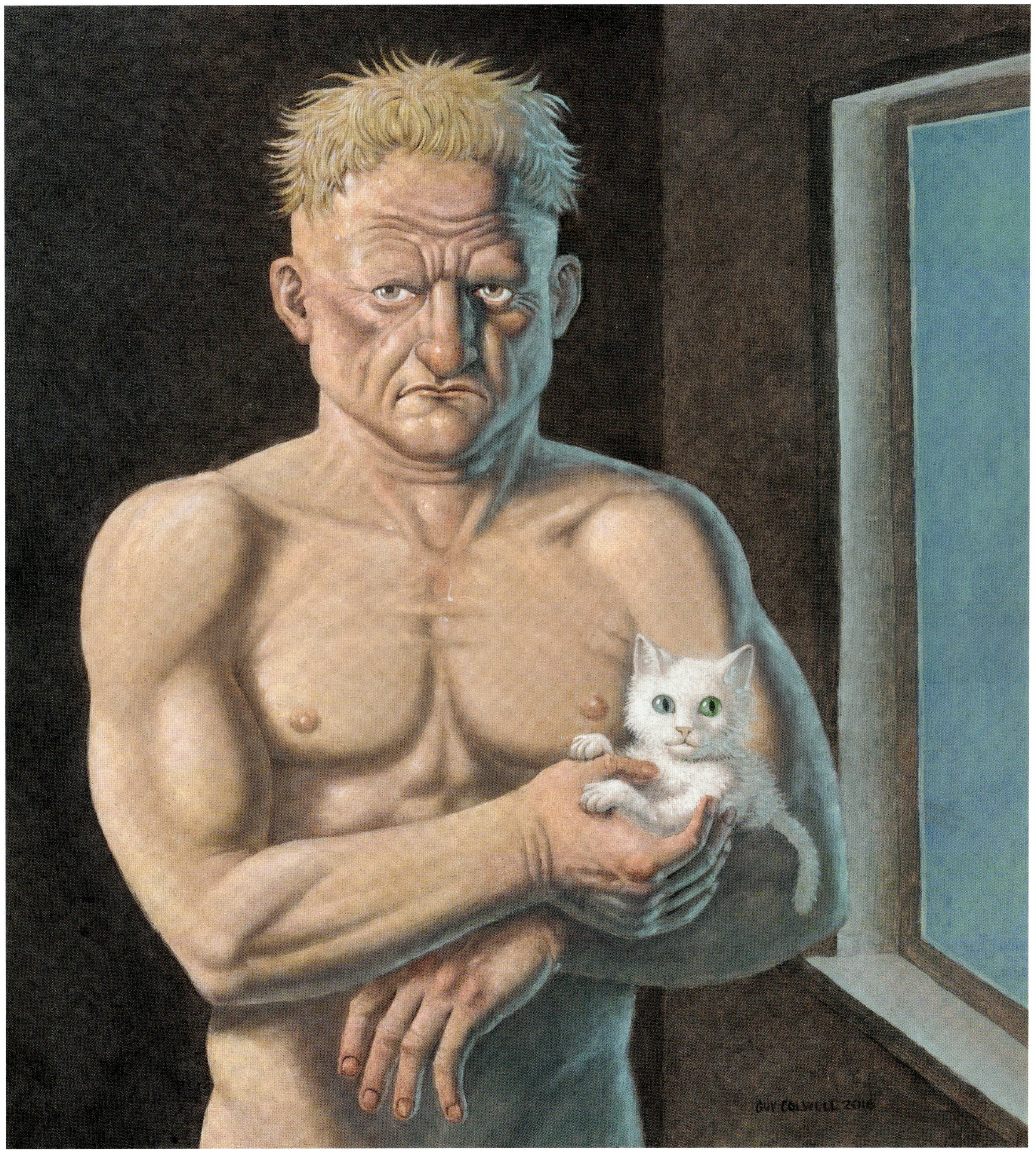

GUY COLWELL 2016

WOMAN ON ROCKS

Oil on canvas • 1991 • 21 × 23 in.
J. Paul Ghetto Collection

I don't do nude paintings with a model in front of me. That would be unworkable because my way of painting is slow and meticulous. A simple painting like this, with a single figure and a visually interesting background, might take two to three months to complete, with several layers of underpainting and several more of transparent glazes. A model wouldn't sit that long, and I couldn't afford to pay for so many hours. But I have a large accumulation of live figure drawings from art classes and drawing workshops I've attended or organized over the decades. Sometimes, one of these saved drawings strikes me as being a good basis for a painting. This is one of those. Painting nudes in natural settings is a thing I do frequently. I try to convey a sense of the bliss I have sometimes felt when deep in wilderness areas when the problems and anxieties, the usual struggles of life, seem just a bit farther away.

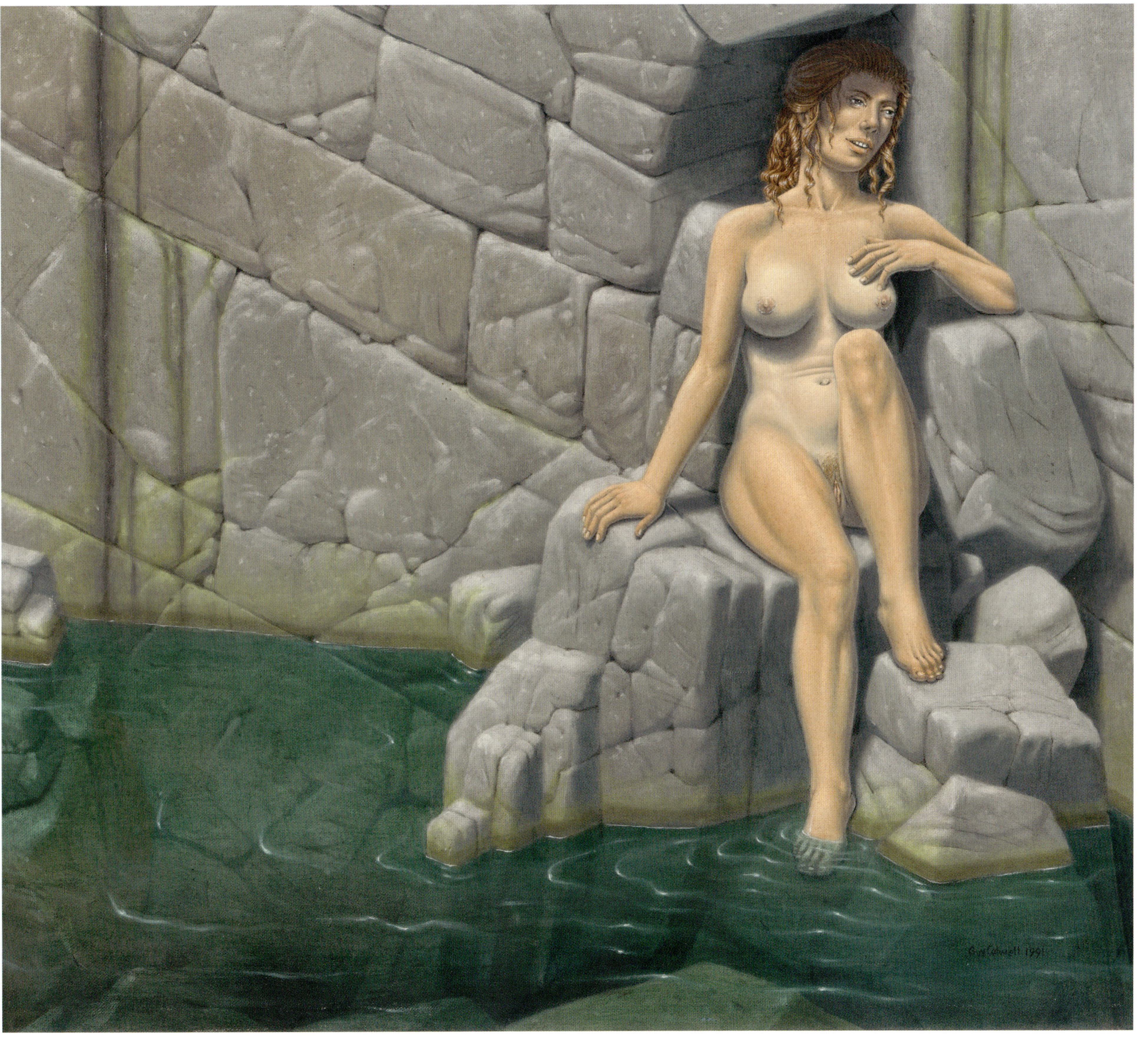

STUDENTS

Acrylic on canvas • 2006 • 38 × 51 in.
Owned by Patrick Dunbar

To study the history, sociology and politics of our species will expose the student to a panoply of horrors. But careful study also shows human progress. There is less legal slavery, more orderly societies living by more and more rational laws. There is more international dialogue and greater interdependence. There are new forms of communication that are breaking down the distances and barriers that have always made humans into strangers to one another. There are fewer and fewer great national wars. In the midst of the persisting horrors, there is reason to hope a better world is emerging. The student who wishes to make a positive contribution to the world has to hold on to this hope and work out some way to avoid joining in the madness that persists.

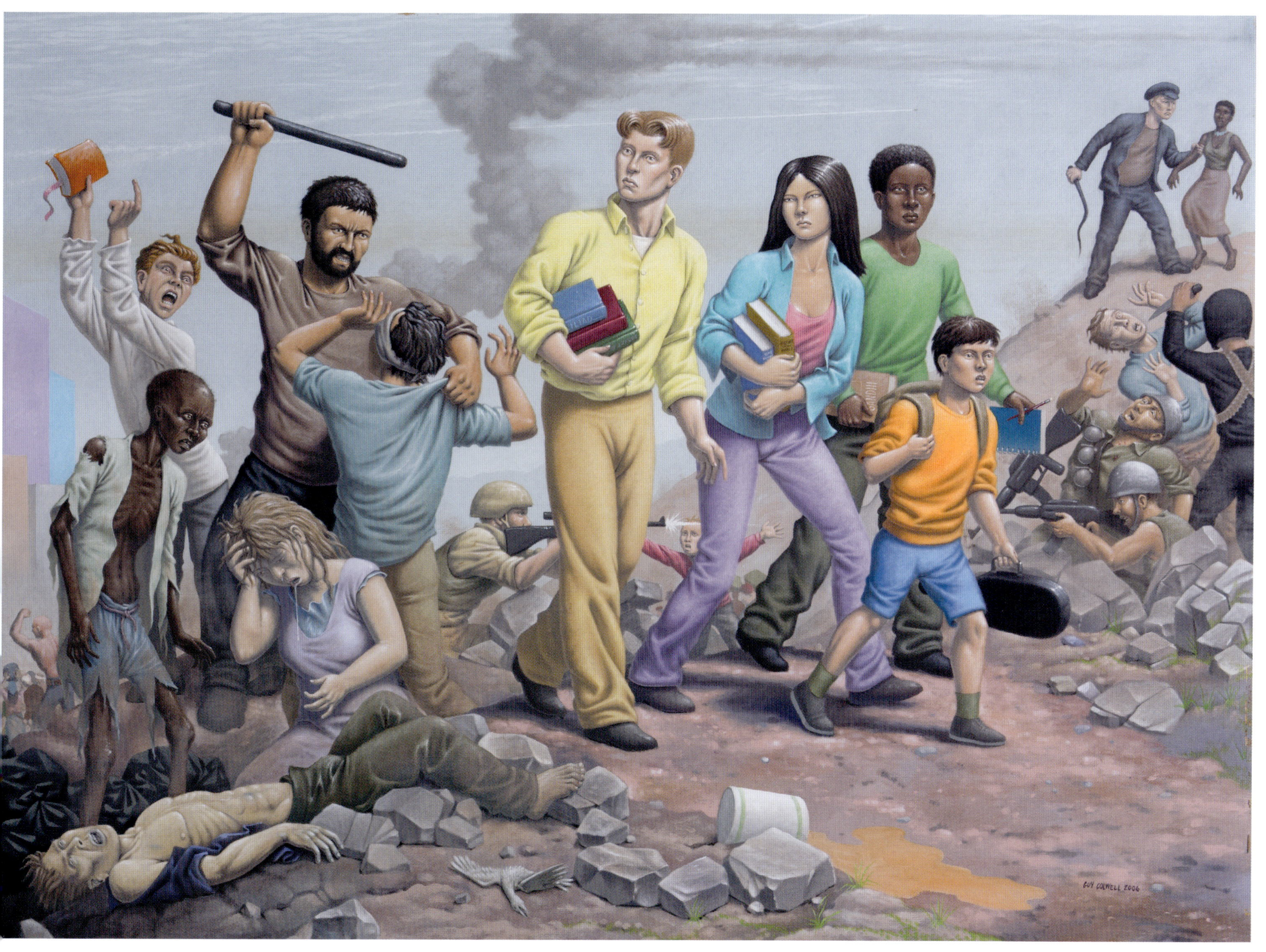

WOMAN AND TIGER

Oil on canvas • 1997 • 23 × 30 in.
Owned by artist

In high school and art school, mid-1960s, I was captivated by abstract painting. Pure form, pure color and expressionism were the commanding approaches of the time, and I went for the ride. But life demanded something else from my artwork when the Vietnam War turned everything upside down and nearly triggered a revolution. I felt compelled to stash the abstract chops away, and turned to teaching myself to be a Social Realist commentator in the tradition of George Bellows, Grant Wood, Thomas Hart Benton, John Sloan, Edward Hopper and others, and I kept this up for the next fifty years. But abstraction is hard to keep down. The simple purity of it is beguiling. From time to time, it flares up, causing brief outbursts of distorted form, color experimentation and out-of-the-ordinary expressionism. This painting represents one of those moments where I applied some of my old non-objective practice to one of my human/animal encounters. Here, I'm saying we may see nature as awesome and beautiful, but nature may see us as food.

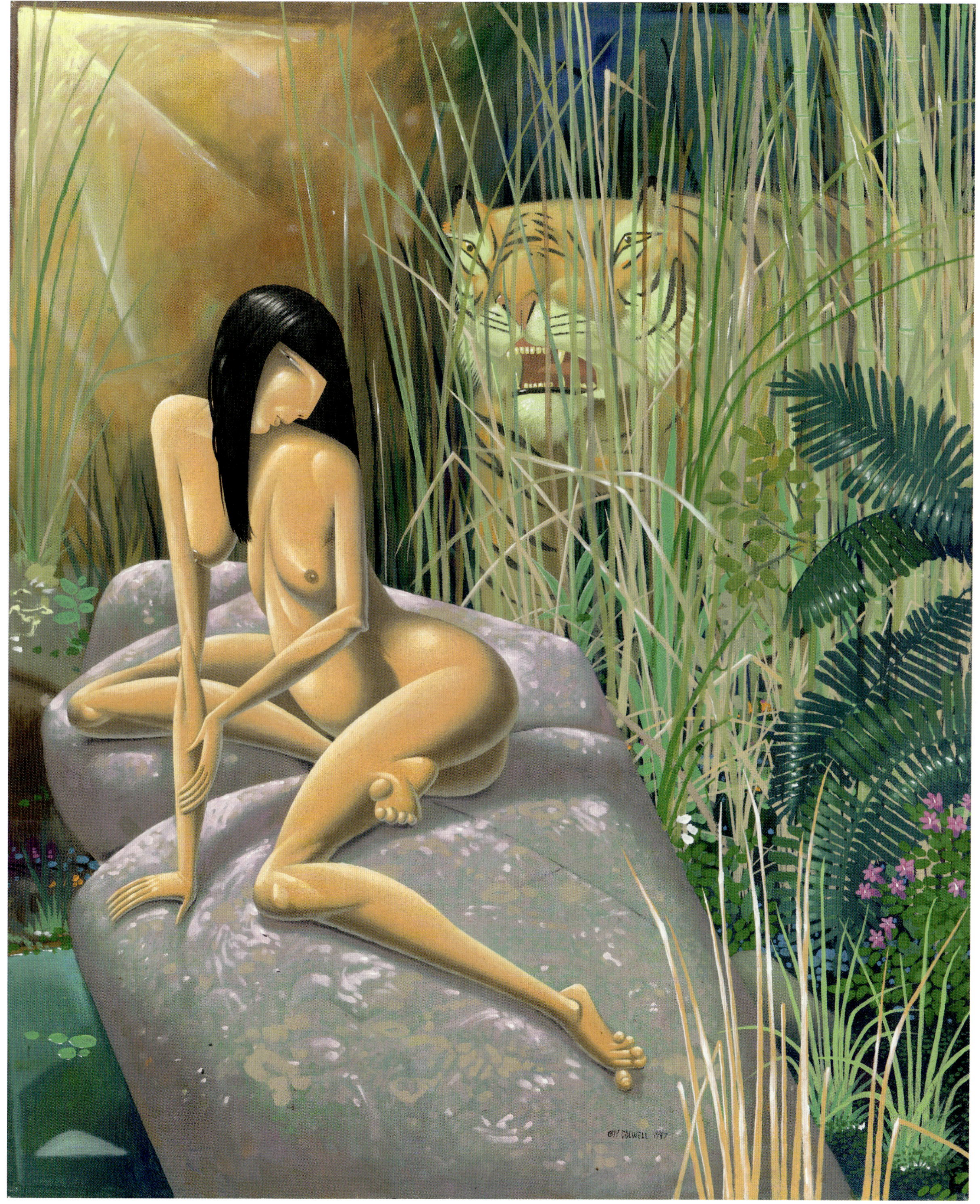

ROY COLWELL 1997

INSTITUTIONAL WARTHOG

Acrylic on canvas • 2005 • 31 × 41 in.
Owned by artist

Here is a woman confronting her fears in the hospital hallway. Perhaps medication will nudge this hallucinatory warthog back into some deeper mental crevice. The natural world, whether it's the one within us or the wild outside places full of danger, is a region that provokes the most profound discomfort for modern city people. We have built a wood, metal, plaster and plastic environment that is isolated from true natural reality. The real world of creatures, trees, rivers, mountains, geologic processes, growth and decay has been fenced off to a great extent from human consciousness. It would be a shocking strangeness to encounter a little of that living animal truth within our sealed space. The paradox is we, ourselves, are products of evolutionary wildness. The animal truth is within us, and, while it may be built over and hidden, it is inescapable. Confronting it in ourselves may even make us a little mad.

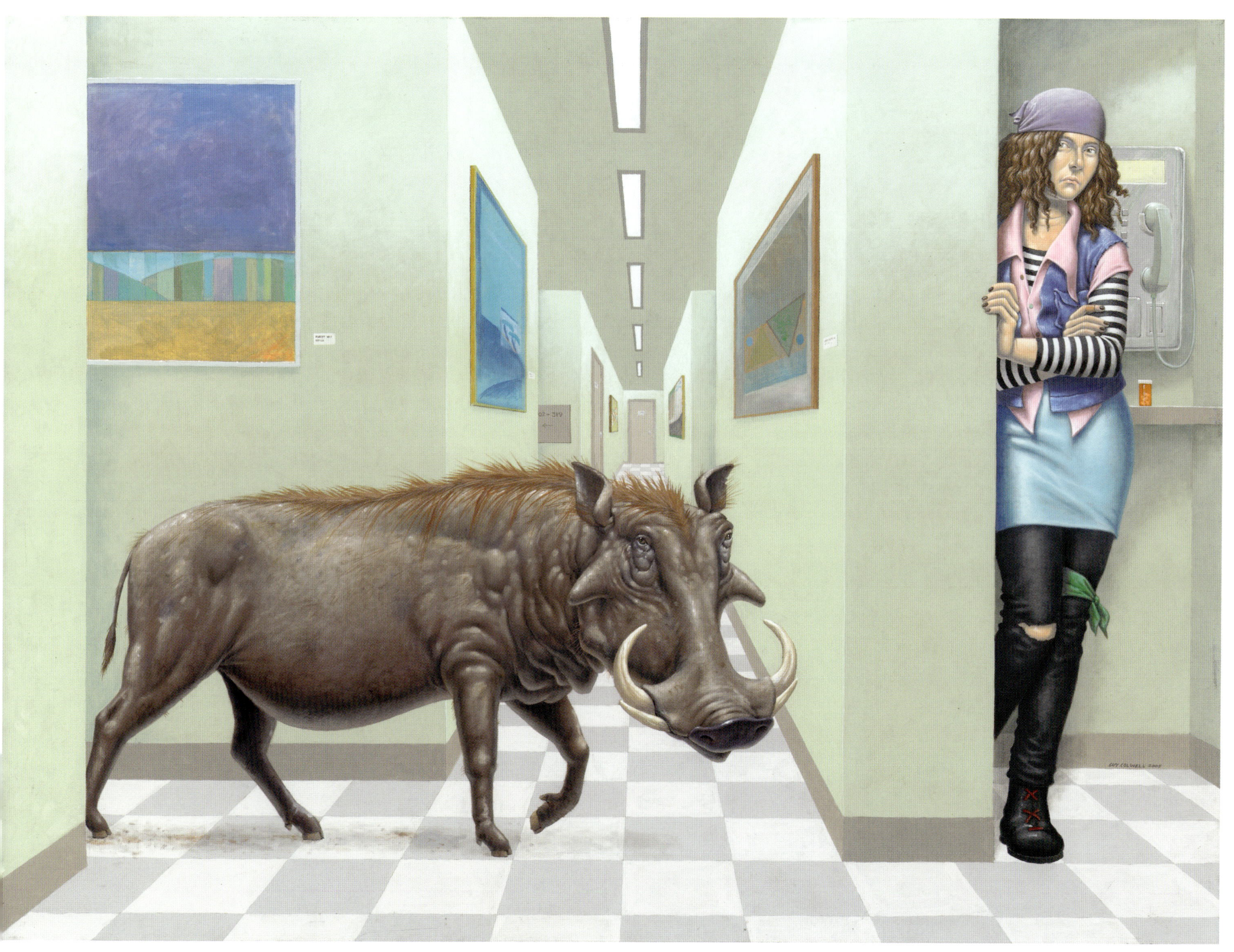

QUIET YOUNG MAN AT VICTORIA FALLS

Oil on canvas • 1992 • 22 × 35 in.
Owned by artist

Here's a painting with an amazing and gentle story about its inception. In my 1990 travels through Zimbabwe, Zambia and Malawi, I carried a sketchbook instead of a camera. One day, in the town of Victoria Falls, Zimbabwe, I went among the locals, away from the tour group, found a place to sit where I could observe the scene and began sketching. To do this in Africa would always attract a group, or sometimes a crowd, of curious onlookers. When they gathered around, I had my pick of faces to record, and the growing crowd was entertained and delighted to watch. I dashed off a few sketches, keeping some I liked and giving others away. One quiet and handsome young man, in his teens, seemed like he especially ought to be sketched. He agreed to sit a few minutes and I started work. When this young man assumed the center of attention in a growing circle of onlookers, all eyes turned to him, and something remarkable happened. The entire crowd around us fell silent… The young man, calm and, well, dignified, radiant, almost angelic, seemed to cast a spell. The boisterous encircling crowd was, for a time, compelled to an awed quiet. It was nothing about my drawing that brought this calm to settle on the gathering — only a few could actually see what I was putting on paper — it was the young man, whose gentle demeanor seemed to touch everyone who looked his way. When I closed my sketchbook, the now-large number of onlookers did not resume any raucous cacophony, but quietly dispersed, each one carrying a bit of this enchanted moment with them. The young man vanished in the crowd without requiring thanks or reward.

I knew I would have to make a painting that combined my sketch of Victoria Falls with my sketch of the young man. And I knew the painting could not come close to containing the unforgettable specialness of this encounter.

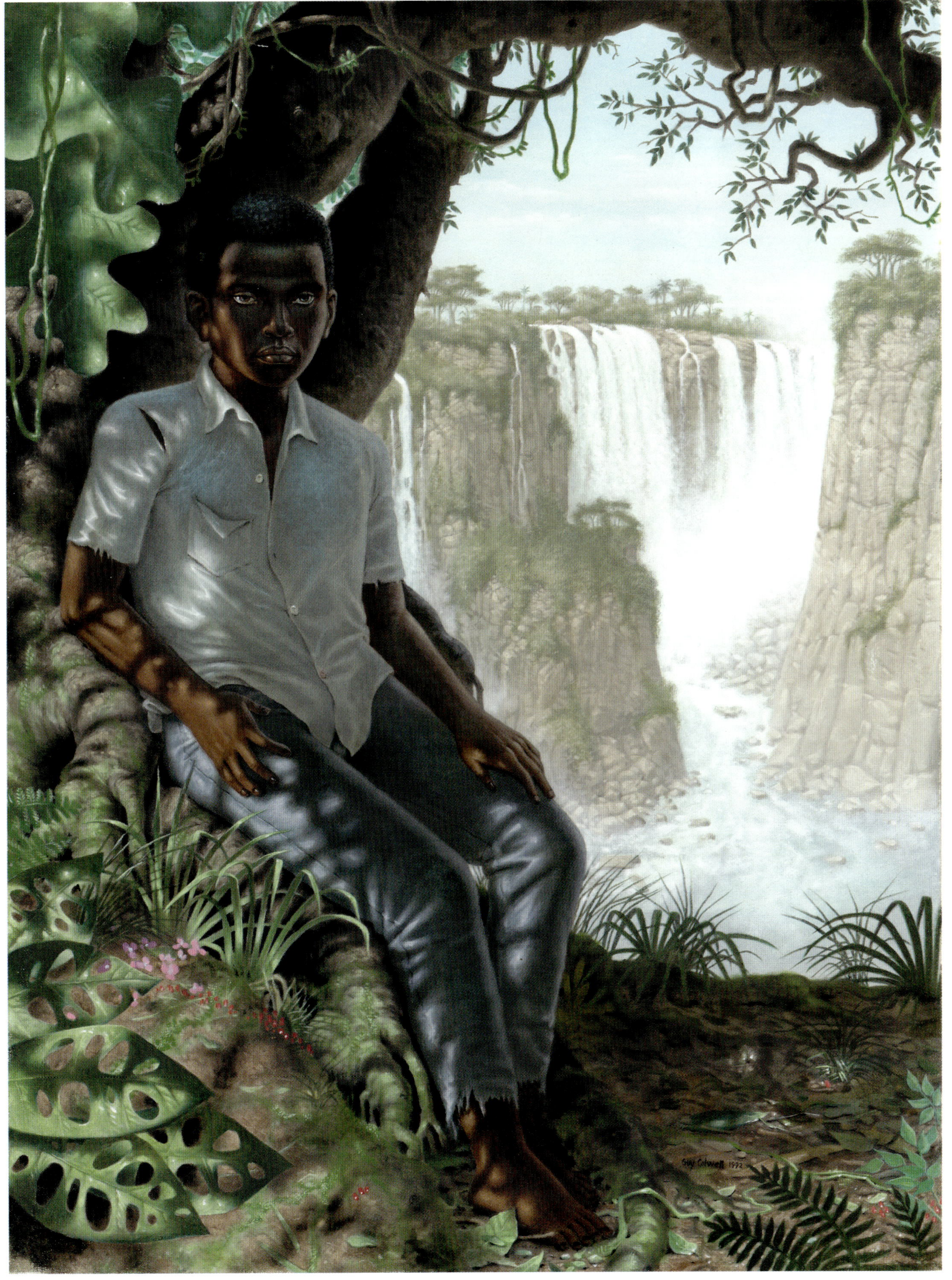

GATHERING BERRIES ON ZOMBA PLATEAU

Oil on canvas • 1992 • 25 × 30 in.
Owned by Andreas Jones

This was a reconstruction of a fleeting impression. I believe we were leaving Zomba Plateau after our multi-day stay-over at this region of Malawi, at a higher elevation than the surrounding open Savannah. It was the sight of a lovely young woman accompanied by two children in a heavily wooded area. They were apparently collecting something that I supposed (for the purpose of my painting) to be berries. They were visible for only a few seconds as we drove past, so I was not able to work on a true likeness. Only try my best, working from a fresh memory and a deep impression, to make something close that got at a feeling of the place and the person. I think I did a good painting, but I did not manage to catch the true beauty of this forest forager.

Zomba reminded me of California. Moderate weather, abundant trees that looked like pine and a mostly laid-back feeling. That is, until President Hastings Kamuzu Banda showed up in his limousine, with a four-motorcycle escort, for the opening of parliament, which happened to occur on Zomba Plateau while we were there. Then, the atmosphere became electric, with hundreds of people crowding the town to greet their authoritarian president for life.

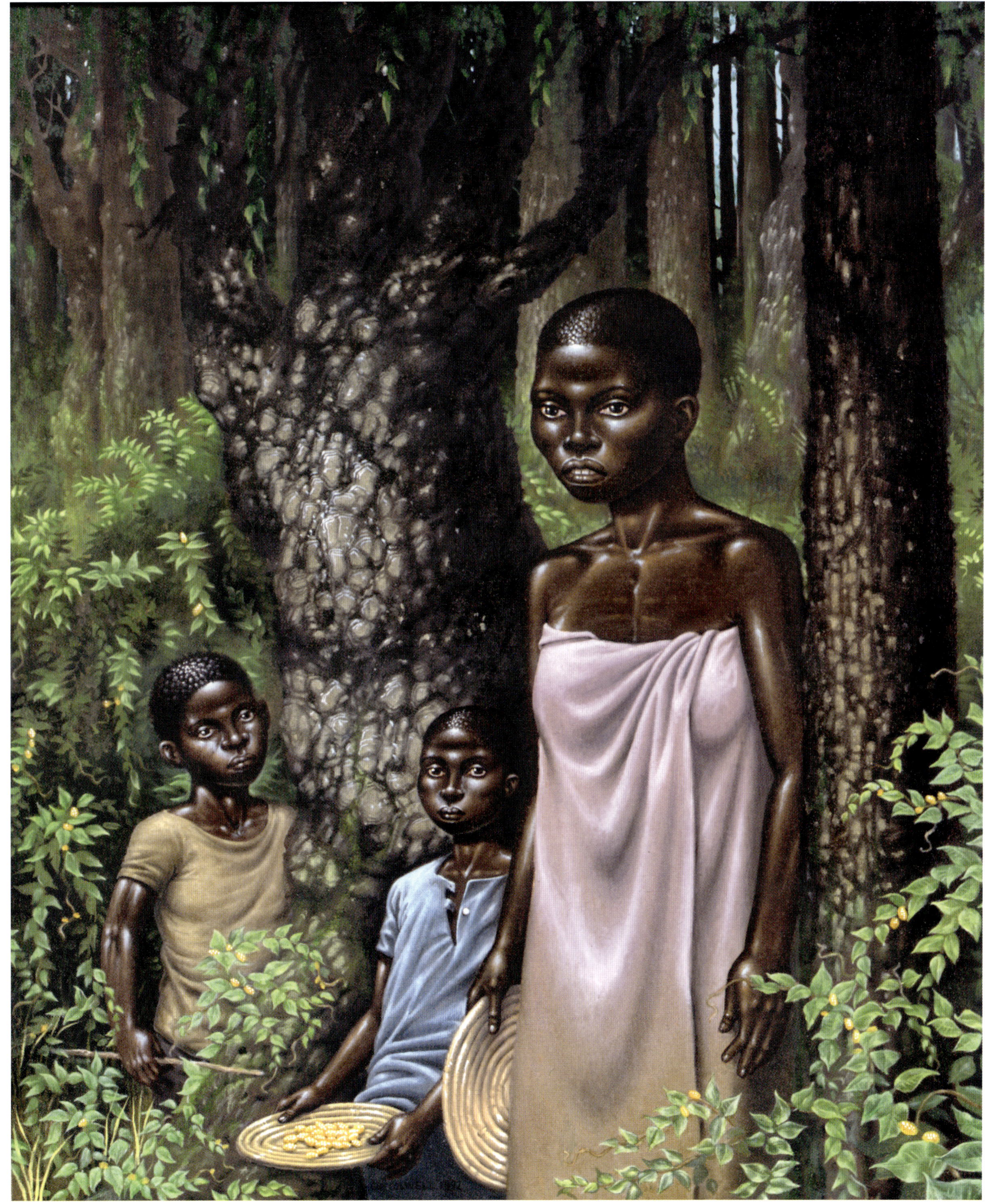

WOMAN AND STRANGLER FIG

Oil on canvas • 1992 • 18 × 30 in.
Owned by Fat Dog

We traveled through Zimbabwe, Zambia and Malawi in an old repurposed British troop truck. I recall sketching this woman while sitting in the truck as it took on gasoline somewhere along the way. At another time, probably during an overnight campsite stop, I sketched a Strangler Fig that was in the slow process of encasing a host tree in a tangle of creeper branches that would eventually kill the host, which will decompose, leaving behind a hollow latticework tree.

I combined these two sketches, refined and transferred them to canvas and worked up this painting. Some of the work I did in the early '90s, including this and others I did after my Africa trip, I consider among the best in my life.

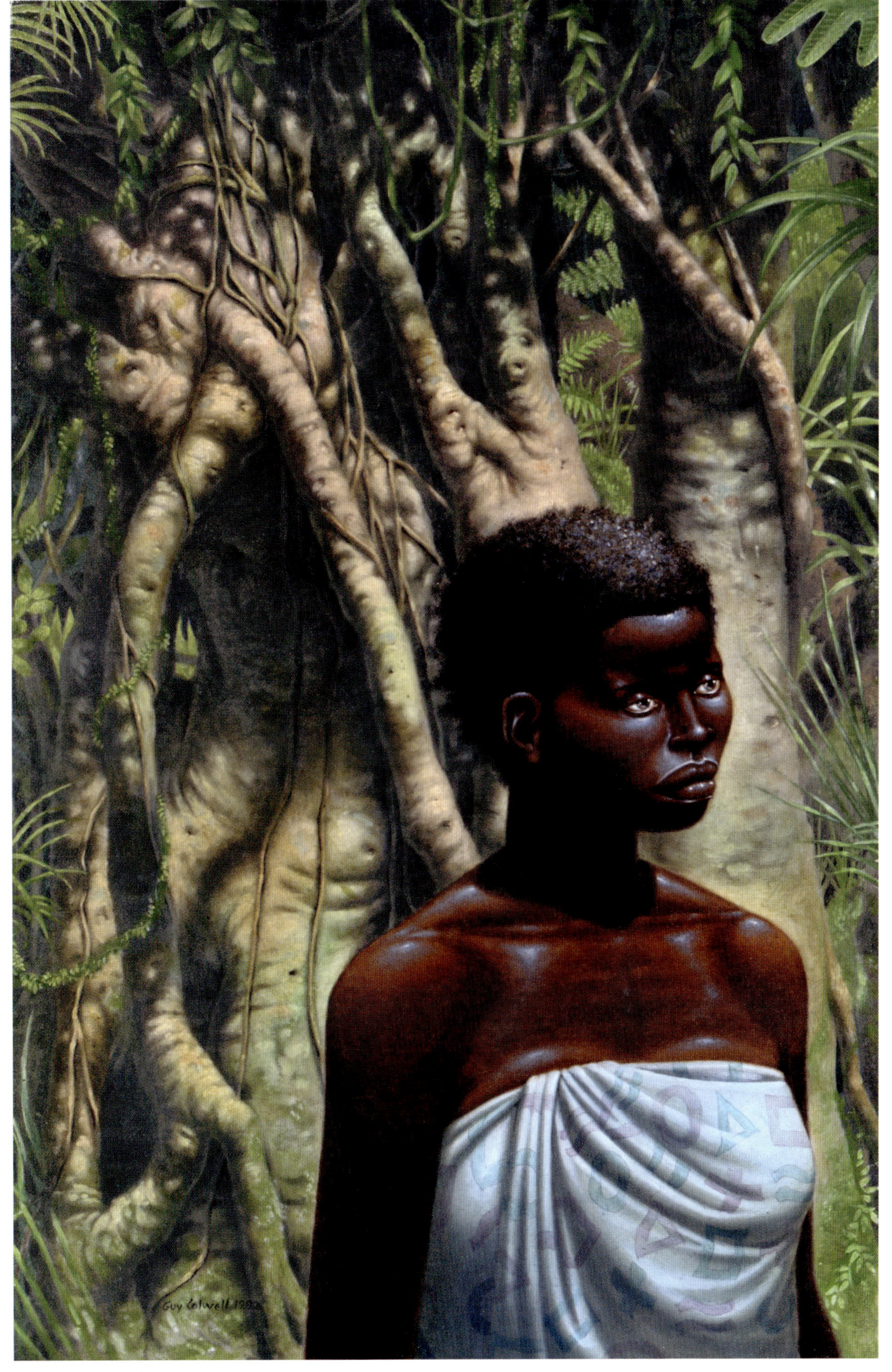

DREAM WEATHER

Oil on canvas • 2021 • 36 × 47 in.
Alex Seastrom Collection

Everything seemed discombobulated, bizarre and even frightening at the peak of the pandemic. It was hard to think straight or have clear certainty about the future, with hourly reports of millions dying — never knowing if it's going to be worse or burn itself out quickly. I tried to get some of this consternation into a painting with glaring color and crowded, incoherent composition. The main purpose was to make it look like a bad dream, and capture that quality with disconnected images of both beauty and terror tumbling over one another. To scan across this jumbled surface would, I hope, reproduce the shifting and transforming quality we find within one of the nighttime dramas our brain produces.

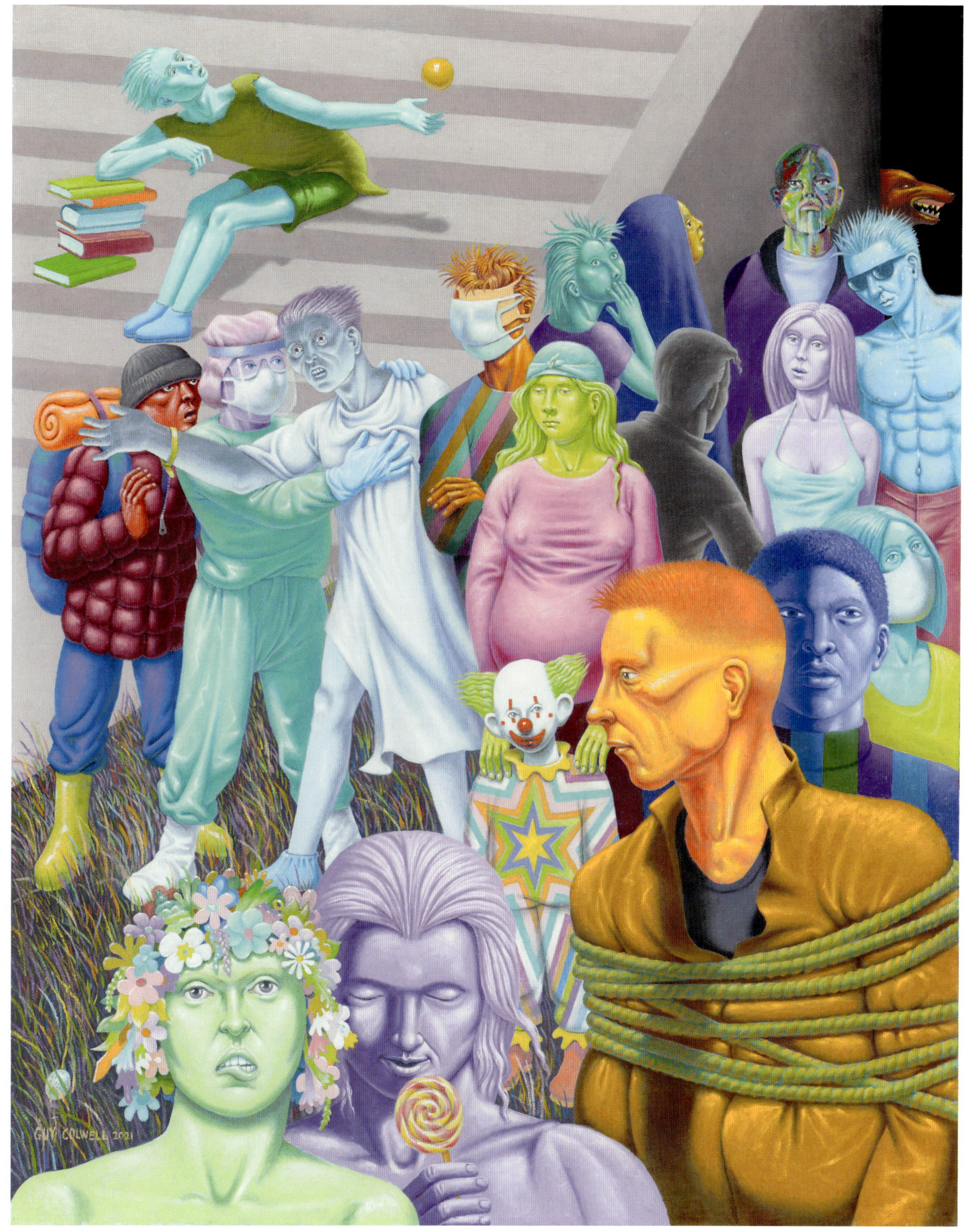

GUY COLWELL 2021

SILENT MUSIC WITH CHORUS AND GRATUITOUS HOOTCHY KOOTCHY

Oil on canvas • 2022 • 30 × 38 in.
Owned by artist

Visual art, without stereo enhancement or other extraneous soundtracks, is silent. So I painted a picture about making music but made it also about silence by removing all the musical instruments. I suppose it makes no great sense, but neither does most surrealism, except as your mind on the subconscious level interprets and entangles it with your dreams.

This is another of my recent pure color, alla prima experiments without glazes to alter the colors. I used a method of contrasting open spaces with tight-clustered groupings suggested by the beautiful work of early Renaissance painter Duccio. I studied how he composed his pictures on a visit to Sienna in 1988. I've carried the lessons with me ever since.

The Hootchy Kootchy babe, however, was not suggested by Duccio.

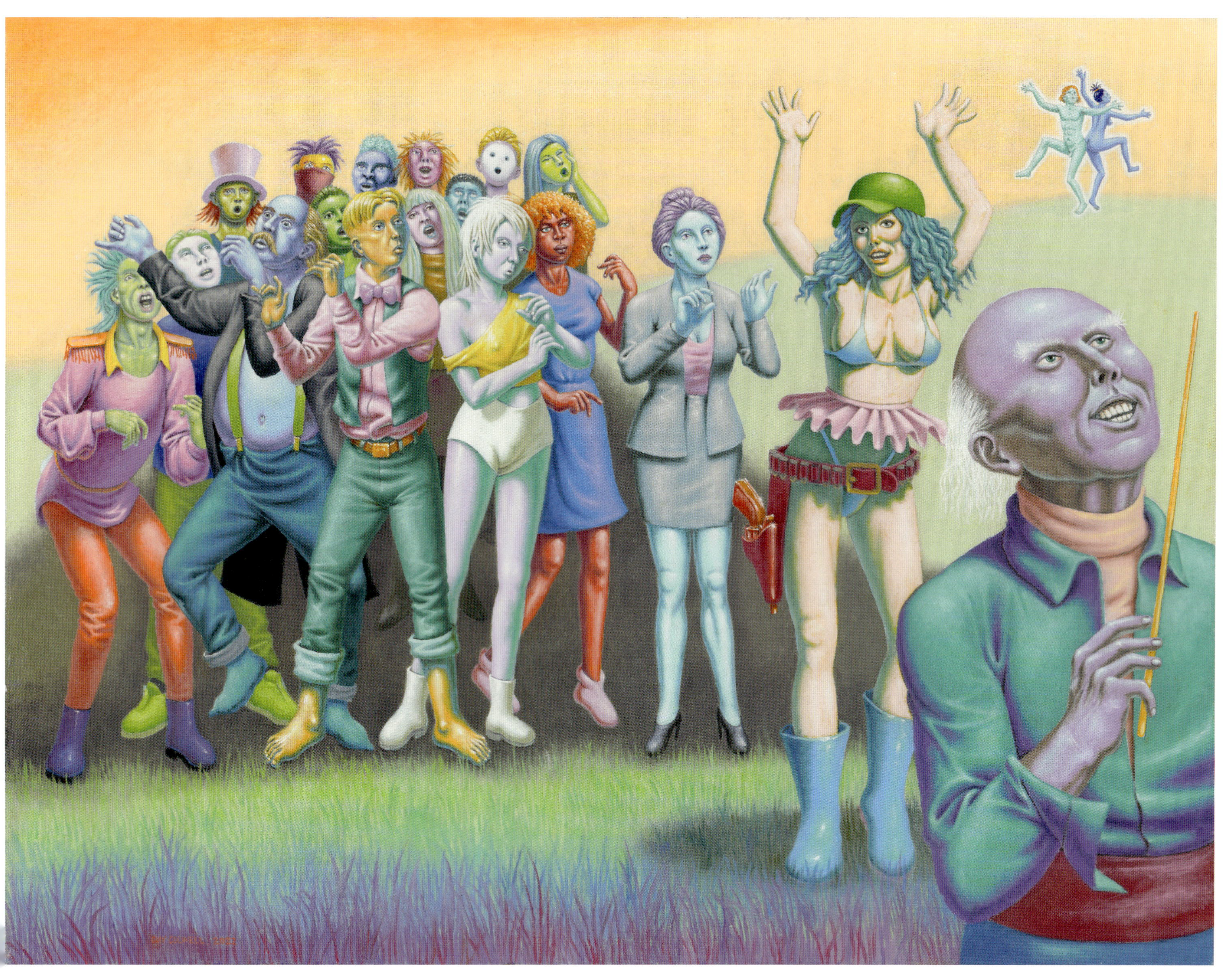

ANOTHER JOKE

Oil on canvas • 2023 • 26 × 42 in.
Alex Seastrom Collection

This is a redo of an earlier painting that had special meaning for me. The first version, called *But a Joke*, had a slightly different color arrangement but essentially the same elements: a sad story accompanied its making.

The last words a special person said to me before being taken by cancer were, "It's so ironic!" This brought to mind the line in the Dylan song, "There are many here among us who think that life is but a joke." That was one of several threads that went into the making of this canvas. Another was a drawing by Picasso of a nude woman, a matador and a dwarf. The matador became the clown, the dwarf became the baby elephant. Some recollection of the delightful circus art of Fernando Botero also found its way into this picture. Another part of it was a reflection on the political climate, where we have one major political party chained to a clown and liable to take a crap on the earth. In a time of personal upset, domestic turmoil and international tension, ridiculous surrealism seemed to be just the right note to sound.

So this "Happy" but surrealistic Clown painting became forever associated with a death, a time of uncertainty and the prospect of chaos and profound change. This second version went deeper into the sadness, with darker shadows and a more corpse-like gray on the young woman.

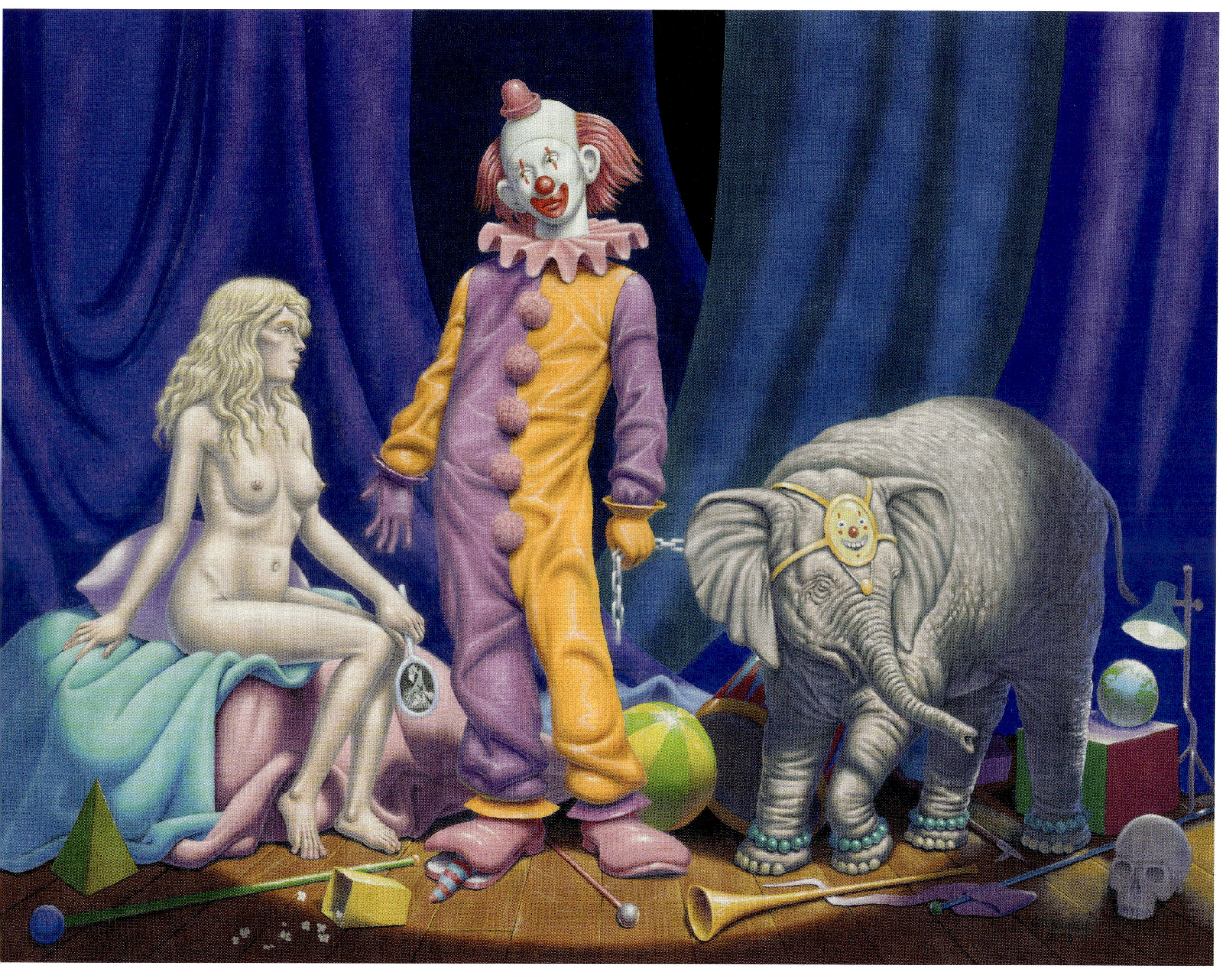

CLOWNS

Acrylic on canvas • 2013 • 45 × 64 in.
Alex Seastrom Collection

This could be comic relief, or the whooping craziness of people trying to make an impression throughout a life surrounded, mostly, by indifference. This is an allegory of a lifetime, with the babe in diapers entering on the left and the figure of death beckoning on the right. We strut through our farcical stories and fret away our little worries from birth to death, and never quite figure out what it's all about.

Paintings of clowns are very appealing, both for the enjoyment it brings to painters as well as the viewers. But somehow, most clown paintings, usually of a single clown face, fall short with respect to having something significant to say. That's why I used clowns to reflect on a larger picture, to suggest life is full of inescapable absurdity, brevity and incomprehensibility. We all trudge along, wearing our happy costumes that distract from the ugliness, and painted smiles to conceal our existential terror and profound ignorance.

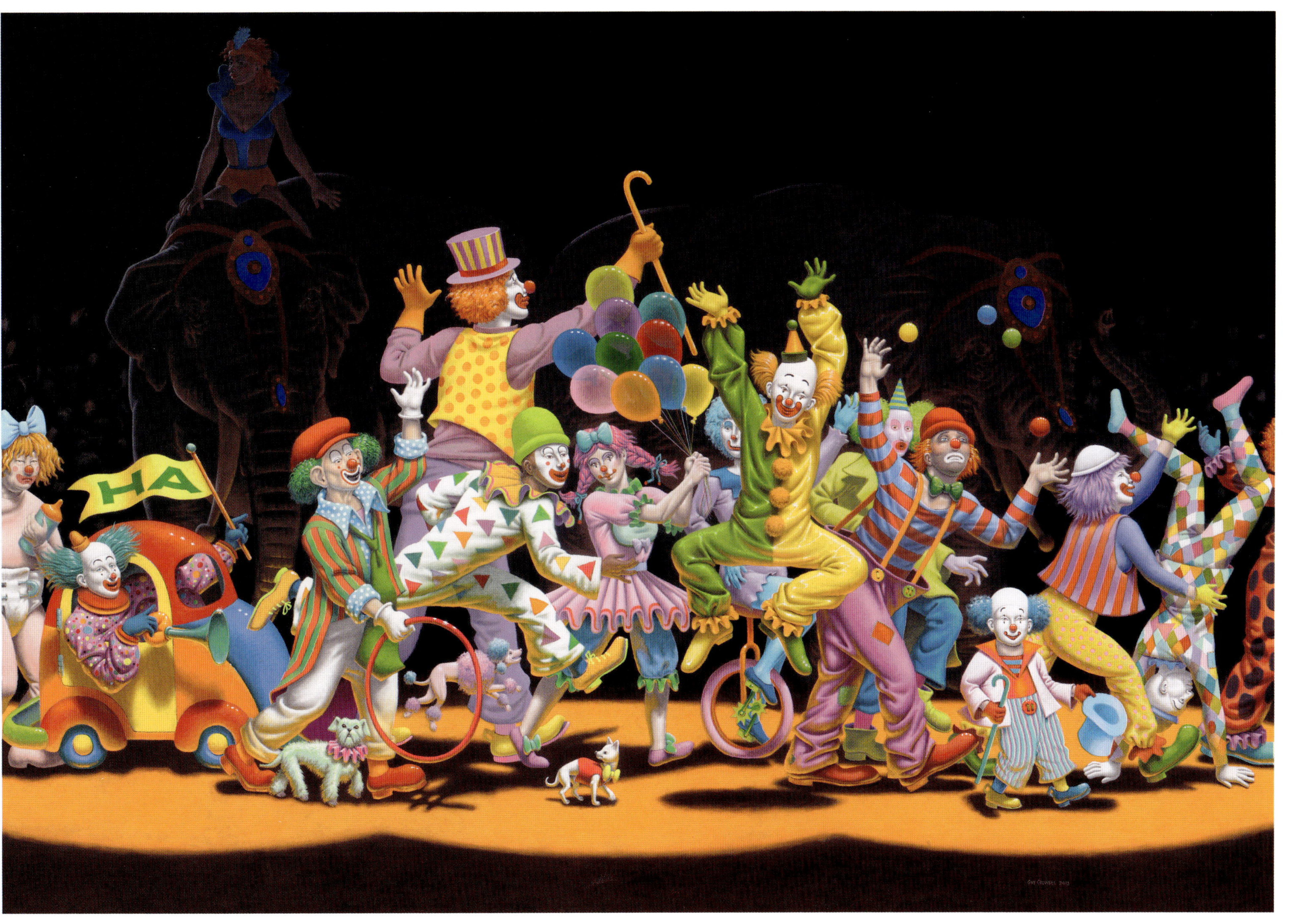
HA

CIRCUS

Oil on canvas • 2022 • 55 × 74 in.
Alex Seastrom Collection

This painting is not based on any actual event that I witnessed. But since posting it on social media, I have been told about incidents of elephants going on a rampage during circus performances. It seemed like a powerful way to represent a confined and controlled animal deciding to revolt against its enslavement to entertainment for an arena full of howling primates. But I also intended it to be symbolic of struggles by human beings against oppression and control.

This big canvas has a history. It was almost abandoned. It seemed too daunting and time-consuming after I put the drawing on the canvas and laid in some initial underpainting. Then I started to let it languish. I had then, as I always do, many other projects and demands on my time. More than a decade went by, and occasionally I would put an eye on the big stretcher frame and consider using it for something else, which would mean un-mounting the unfinished canvas or painting over it. One day, I mentioned this to my wife, who said she would take it away from me if I ever talked about ditching it again. Good thing, because when I showed how much I had done on it so far to collector Alex Seastrom, he immediately commissioned me to finish it. After a few more months of avoiding this difficult undertaking, I strapped in and got it done.

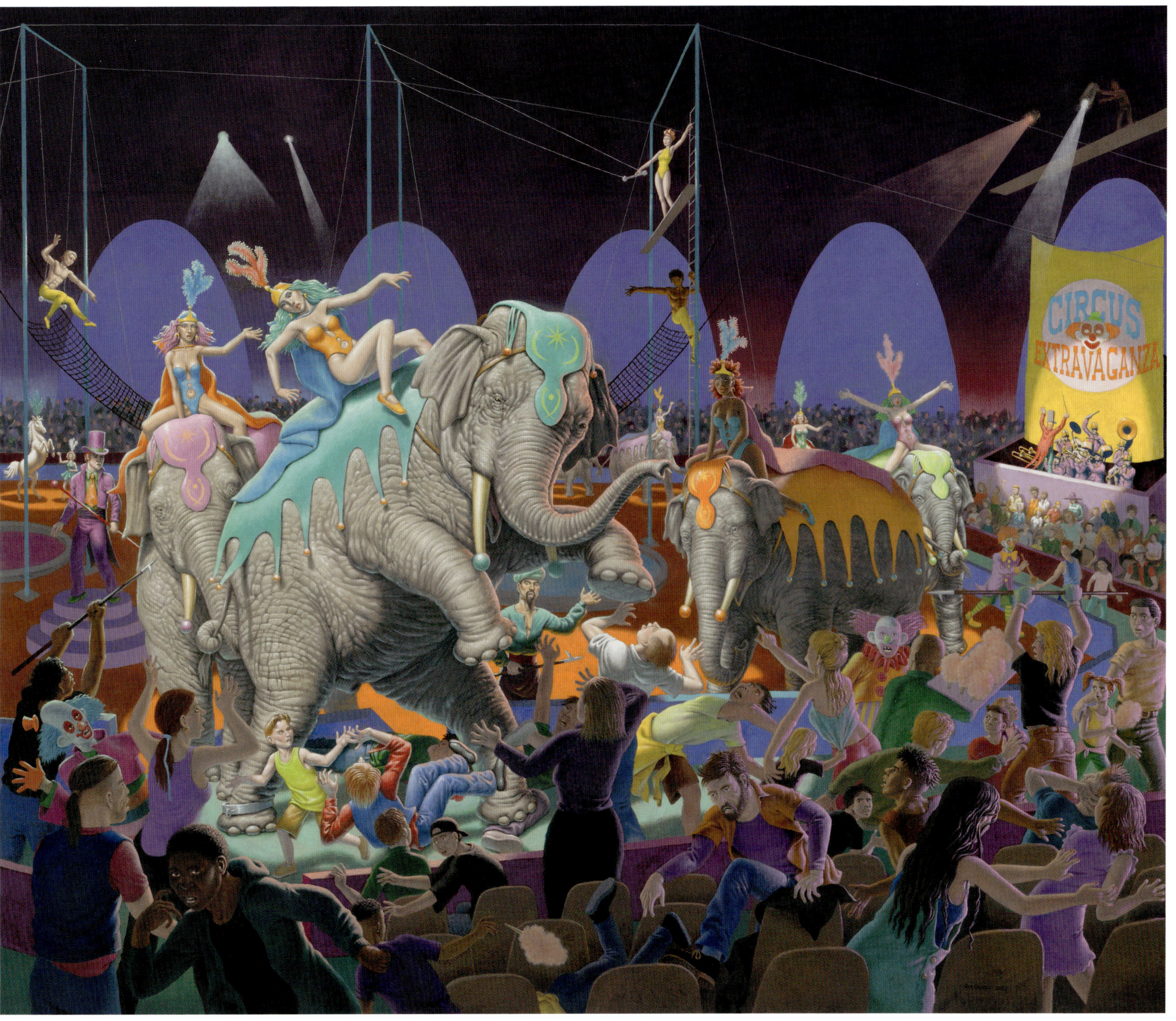

CIRCUS
EXTRAVAGANZA

PEACE TALKS

Watercolor • 1987 • 13 × 17 in.
Owned by Jaime Valdez

The term Figurative Social Surrealism applies most accurately to this painting. The only watercolor included in this book, it was done shortly after completing a 3,000 mile, Coast to Coast march to demand action on reducing the threat of nuclear war. I think the image suggests the thought that throughout our violent and chaotic history, some people have loved making war and some others want to talk peace, write laws that make the world a place where fear of obliteration by sword, gun or bomb is no longer possible. It is my view that the peace-talkers and lawmakers are creating institutions and channels of communication that are making irreversible gains in bringing about a safer world, and war is in the course of ultimate extinction.

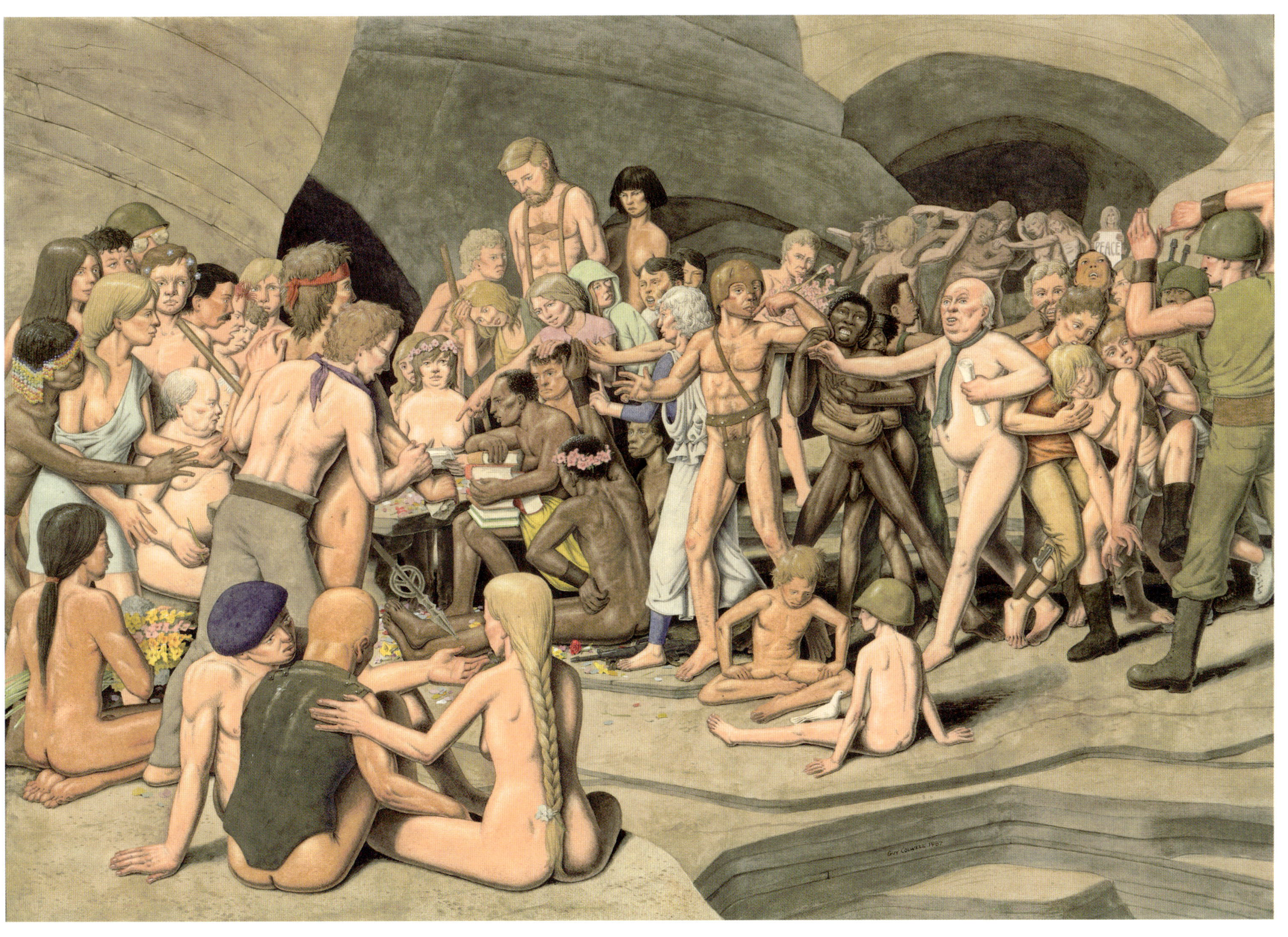

STYLIN' YOUTH REDEFINE THE MEANING OF SKIN COLOR

Acrylic on canvas • 2003 • 30 × 41 in.
Ryan O'Connor Collection

Did you ever think what the world would be like if we could change our skin color as easily as we can our hair color? The very meaning we so often attach to this surface quality may become deeply altered. A white person might try being Black, or a Black person white. Shades of pink and brown might give way to vivid experiments in blue and purple, red and turquoise. Perhaps the widespread use of this new tinting technology would lead to old concepts of color and race becoming lost or obsolete.

This is one of my first experiments using a single, abnormal color for a figure in a painting. I repeated this approach many times during the following decades. It pulled me away from trying so hard to always do rigid reality, and opened up new pathways of experimentation.

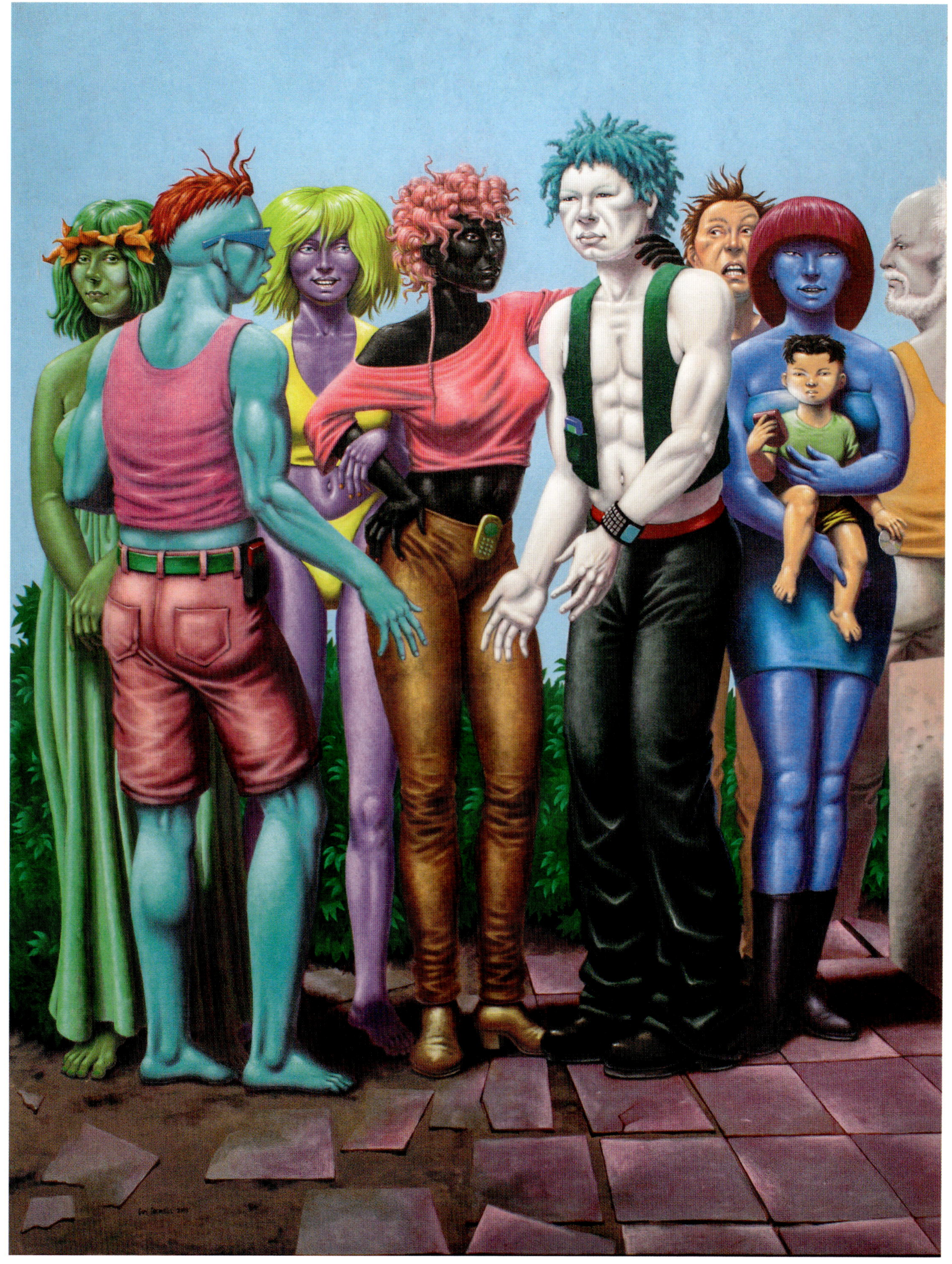

PETROLUCRE

Oil on canvas • 1991 • 30 × 35 in.
J. Paul Ghetto Collection

The first Gulf War ended in 1991. Saddam Hussein had lit up the oil wells in retreat. Red Adair was sent in and put out the fires in short order, which probably had a higher priority than the needs of the people or of rebuilding. So, many people felt it had been a war about oil, who controls it, where it goes in the world, rather than having to do with justice or principle. I imagined the oil magnates in control of other supplies were delighted that the wells were burning, because it meant shortages would make prices rise and they would be all the richer. I had to make some commentary on these events, so naturally I painted a picture.

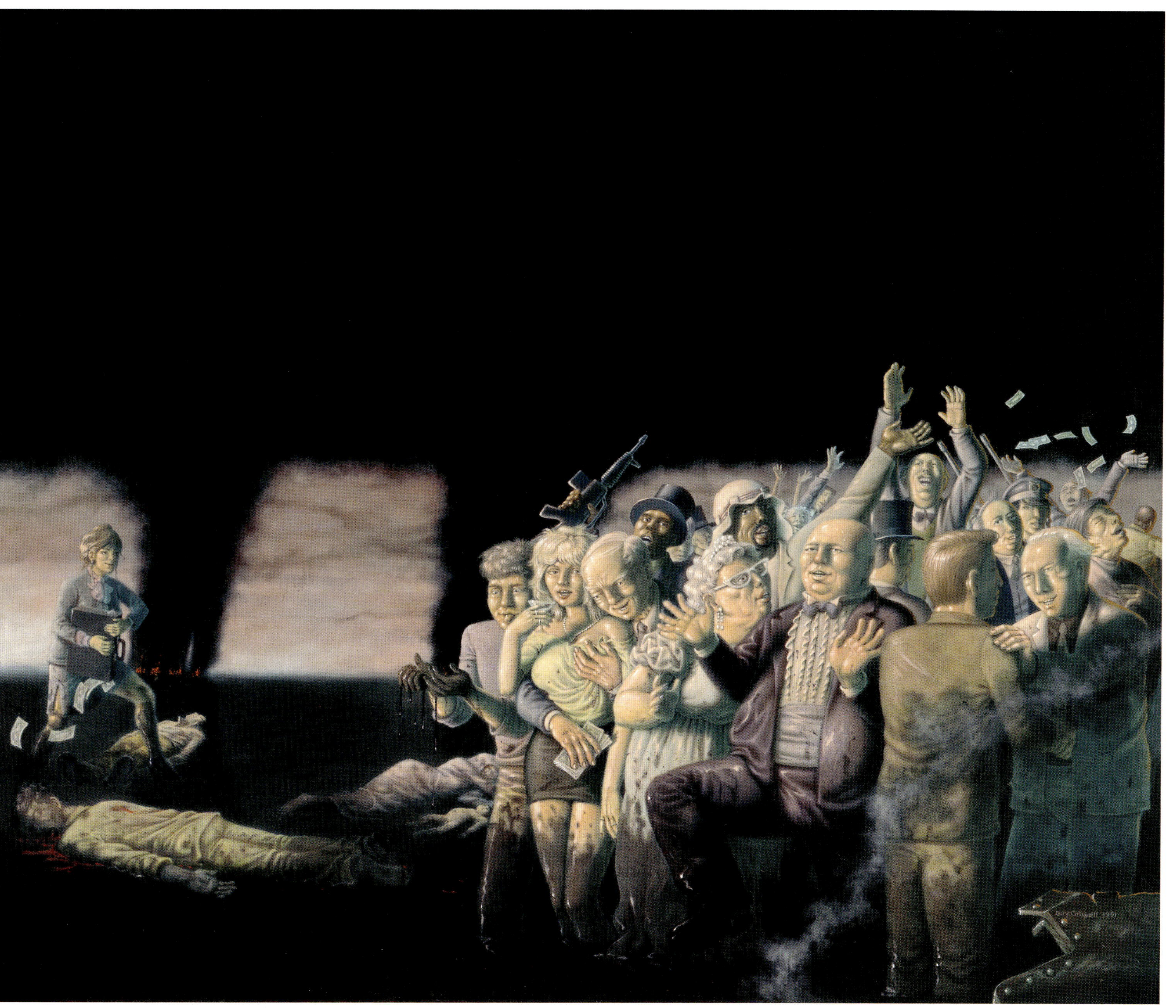

MELLOW BEACH

Oil on canvas • 2023 • 47 × 68 in.
Alex Seastrom Collection

The L.A. surfing kit entrepreneur, Alex Seastrom, asked me to paint him a beach scene. Doing this picture gave me an opportunity to make some points about Global Warming. I felt I had to do this after a couple of summertime visits to family in Arizona where, for the first time in my life, I experienced temperatures in the 110–120 degree range. Brutal. It seems the climate scientists are forecasting this level of heat more often, for longer periods and in more places. So all the bodies here are shown dangerously burned, and a cell phone shows an ambient temperature of 113 degrees. Since 2023 averaged out to above the upper limit recommended by climate science, we had better be prepared to adapt as the weather pushes higher and higher to levels we have all never before experienced. But I have no doubt the people who love the beach will continue seeking the heat, the extra dark tan and the mellow company.

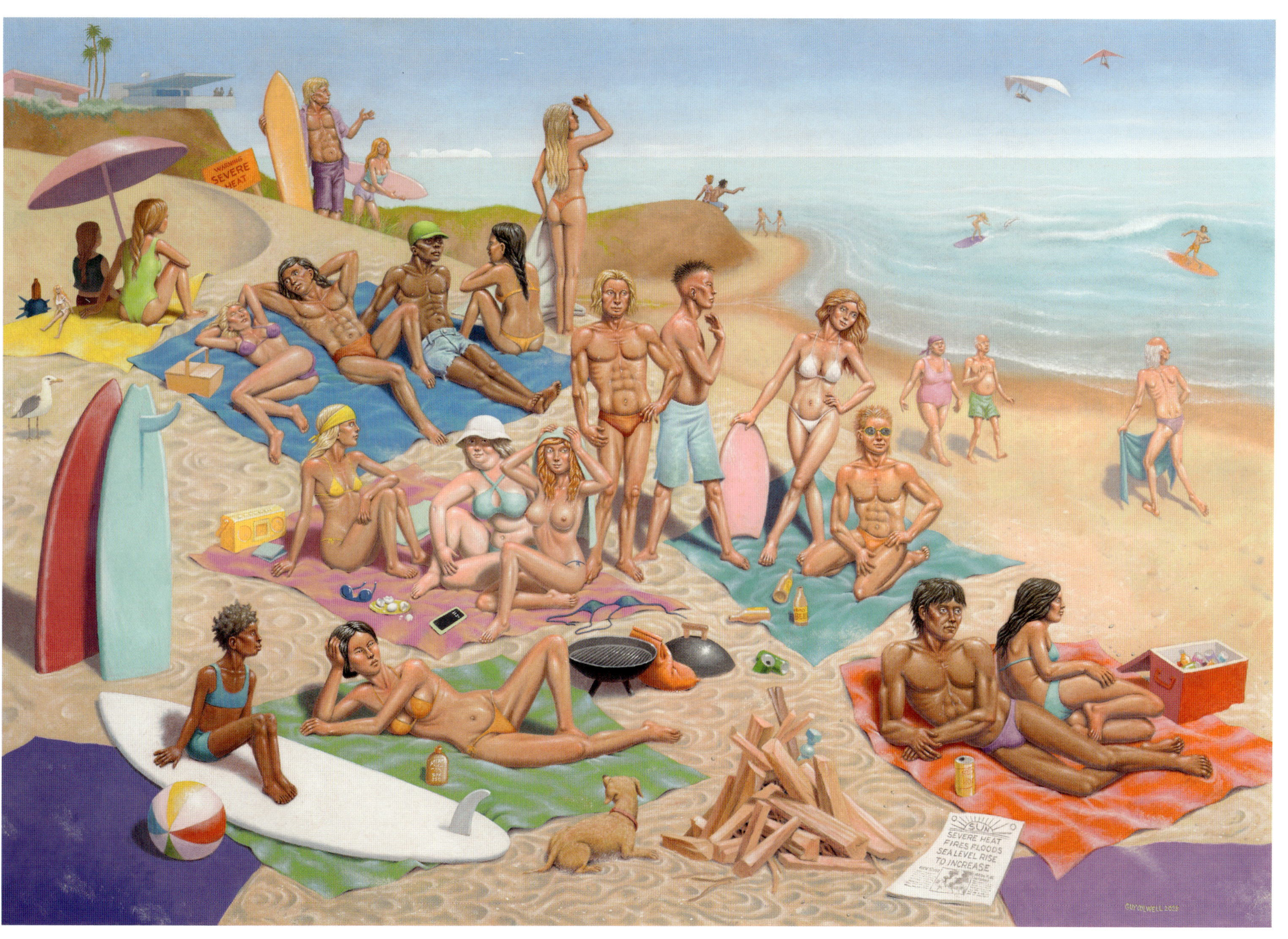

WARNING
SEVERE
HEAT

SUN
SEVERE HEAT
FIRES FLOODS
SEA LEVEL RISE
TO INCREASE

SATURDAY NIGHT SELFIE

Oil on canvas • 2020 • 26 × 37 in.
Ryan O'Connor Collection

She's liberated, or, well, she's an exhibitionist — or maybe she's just stoned out of her brain. If I were in this club watching this young woman display her beautiful young body to all onlookers, I would be swept by strong conflicting emotions. My eyes might not be able to pull away from her. The evolutionary programming demanding an immediate response of sexual arousal would be strong. But could I disregard all the other emotional, intellectual and social imperatives that are also deeply ingrained? I would have to ask myself: does this behavior fit the circumstances of our lives. We are not living in a rule-free Garden of Delight. While she is stripping down and grooving on the attention, somewhere in the world bombs are falling, children are starving, populations are migrating to escape misery or persecution. Perhaps a world of casual freedom will somehow emerge in a few more century… or millennia. But maybe keeping a lid on the frivolity might be somewhat more appropriate while the planet is in dire pain and peril.

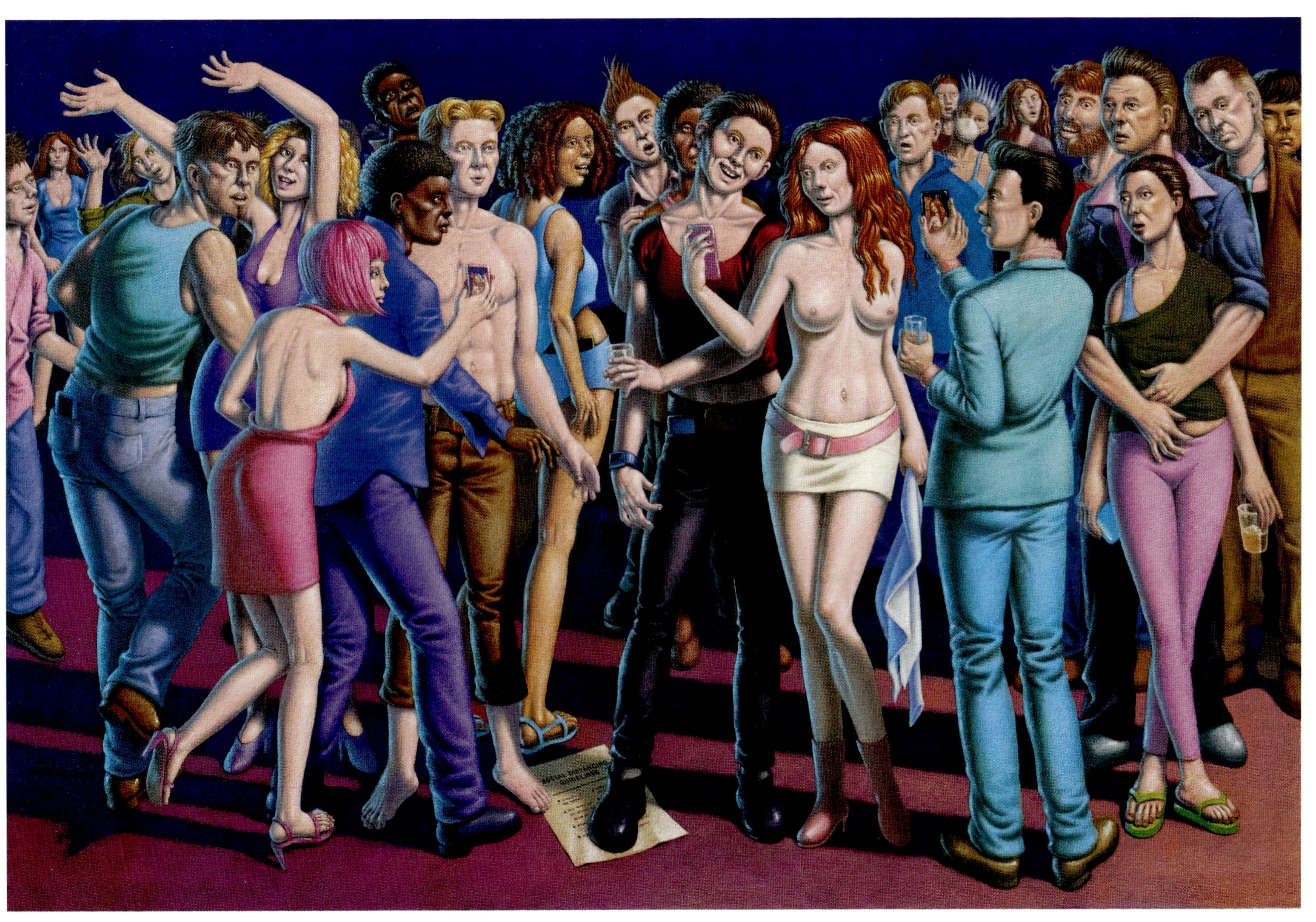
SOCIAL DISTANCING
GUIDELINES

JUNIOR AND THE LEGS

Oil on canvas • 2023 • 19 × 21 in.
Alex Seastrom Collection

From time to time, I do a painting that tries to capture something I've seen in a dream. The dream this was based on stuck in my mind and demanded to be pictorialized. I saw a young man, first in closeup, playing a guitar and singing. The song sounded like Roy Orbison's "Crying," but the dream was writing entirely new lyrics, which of course passed quickly and were forgotten. As he sang his sad song, the point of view slowly pulled back. The young man, who, in the dream, I knew went by the name Junior, could be seen full-figure. And next to him, from an opening in the stage floor, were a number of lovely female legs, just as pictured here. I have no idea if this means anything, but I thought it made an arresting image.

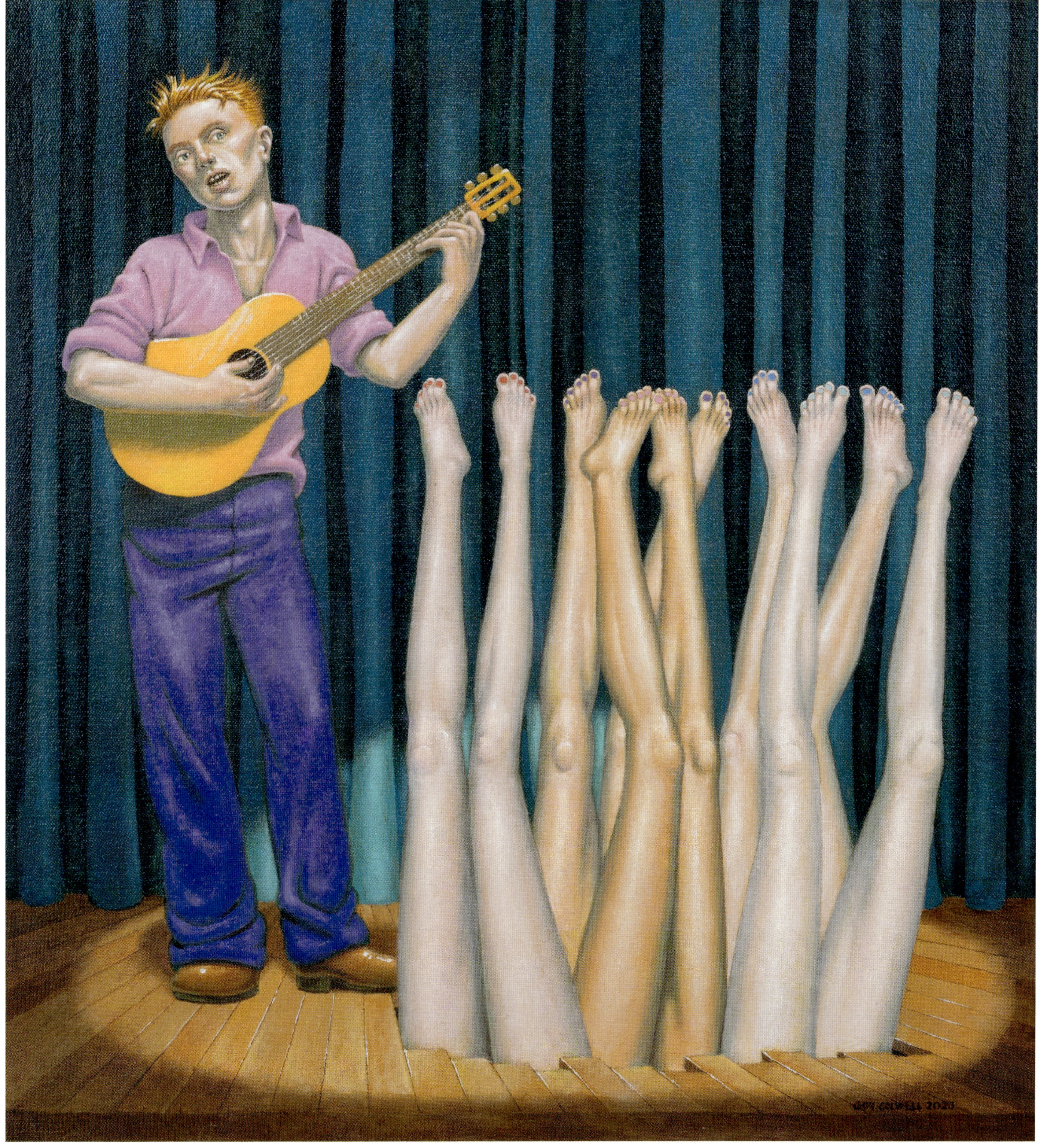
GUY COLWELL 2023

WOMAN ON A BIGHORN

Acrylic on canvas • 2002 • 22 × 27 in.
Owned by artist

Here the mountainous habitat where the Bighorn sheep can be found has become a city skyscraper, and the setting for this surrealistic meeting of wild animal and human female. People still think we are "in the saddle" as the dominant species on the planet. Yet, we know to survive for long in their world would be beyond our capabilities.

We are no longer wild animals, and, for all of our clever inventions, tall buildings, deadly weapons and mastery over nature, we are just big, weak, slow apes without natural defenses. I wouldn't want to encounter a Big Horn sheep in the wild because even these vegetarians would be capable of destroying any unarmed one of us. So this picture is a fantasy of control, a young woman mastering wildness. Possibly meaning her "horny," aggressive boyfriend?

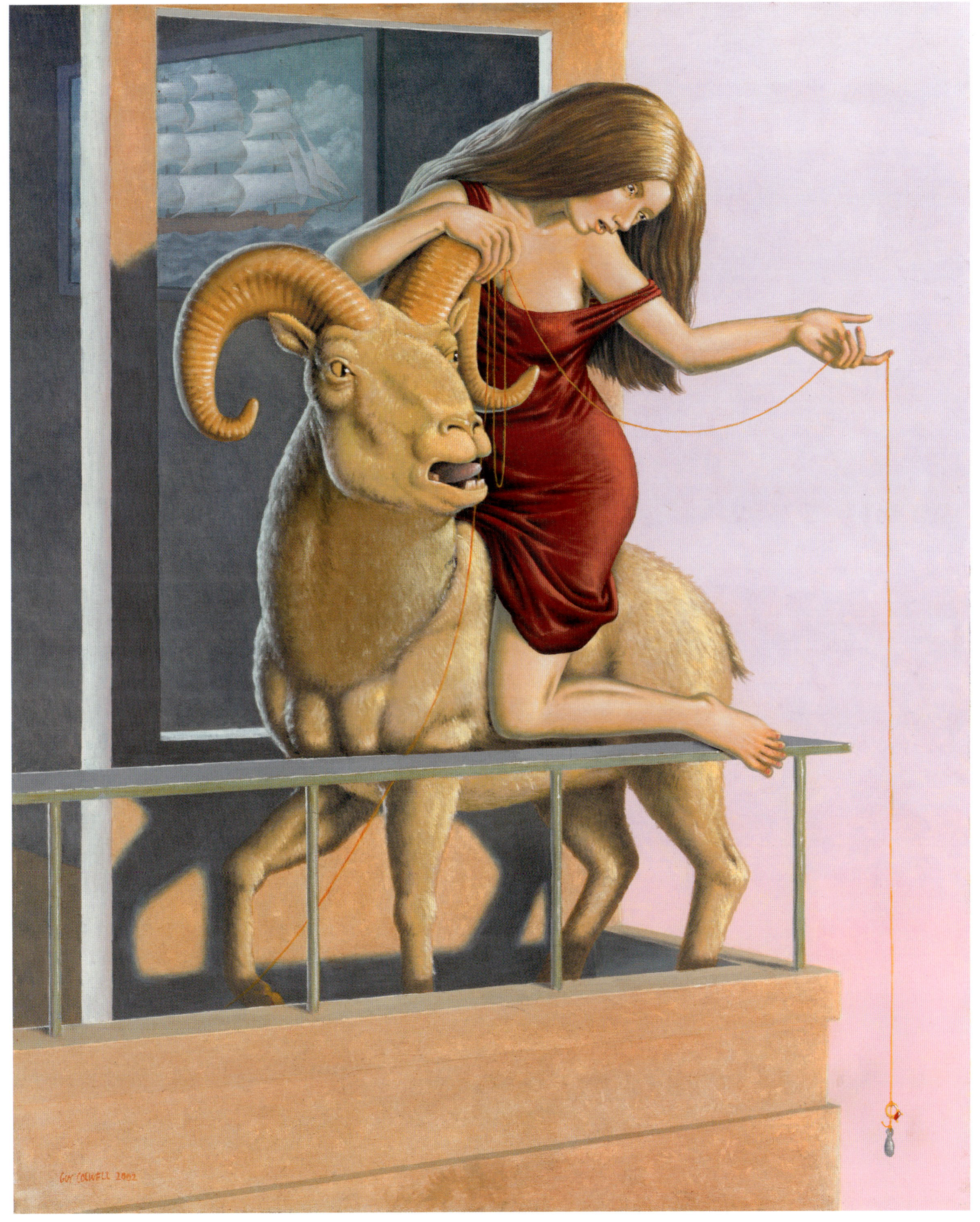
Guy Colwell 2002

SMASHING

Oil canvas • 1991 • 28 × 38 in.
Owned by the artist

It may sound strange, but I think of this man smashing everything made by human hands to be engaging in a kind of Zen meditation. Searching for the fundamental reality, the very ground and core of existence, he wants to cast away all distractions and attachments, clear out all artificiality and get at... something... some thing.... That he hopes is there, and he hopes is real. The bare naked truth, not of things — it's all just stuff — but in just Being when there is no more having.

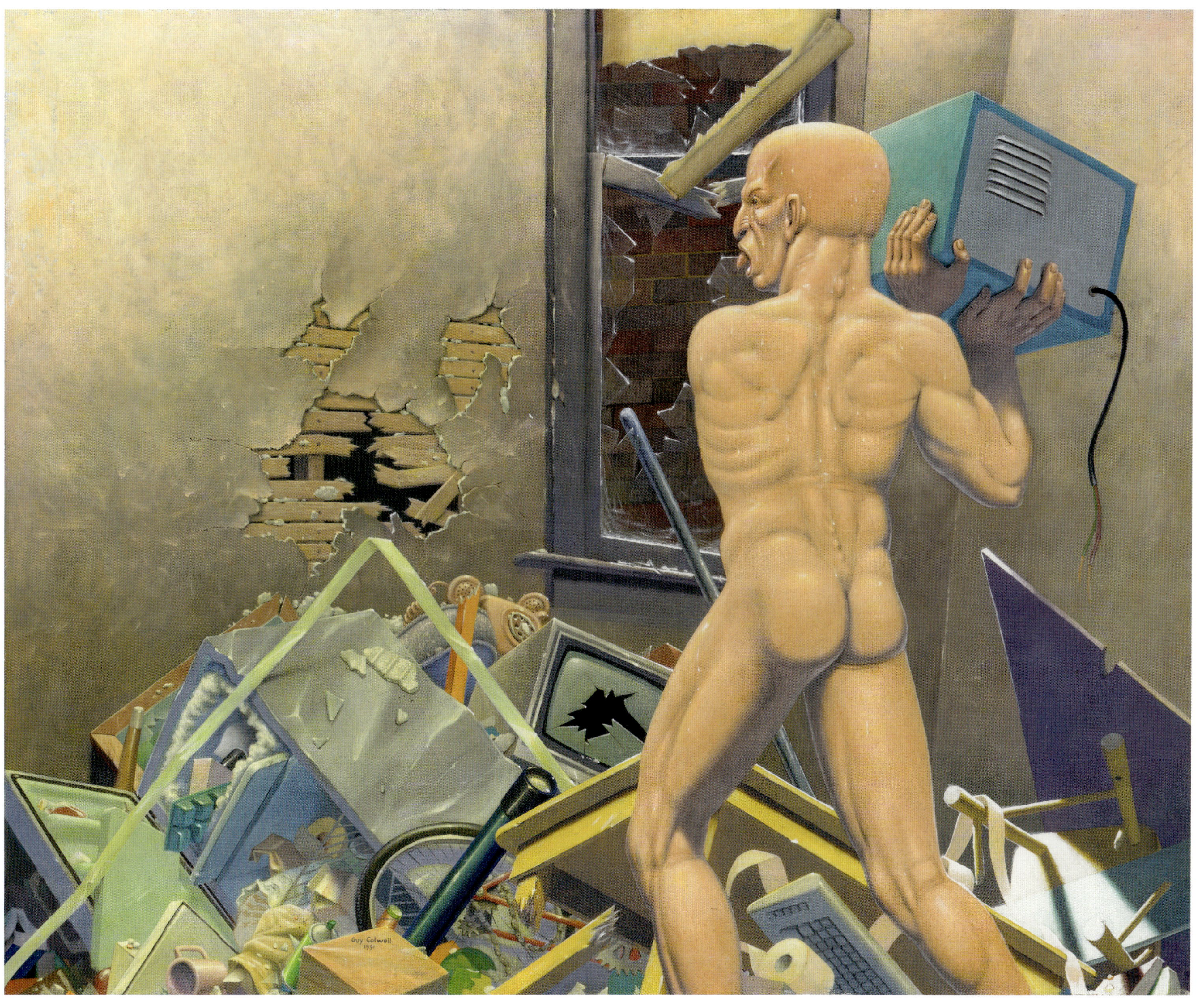

NUDE SIX

Oil on canvas • 1991 • 24 × 35 in.
Owned by artist

Six nude figures based on life drawings done in figure workshops. There is no particular relationship between the people. It's just an appreciation of the beauty, complexity and diversity of the human body. I know I never got as trained up in drawing, painting and anatomy as I could have been. The Vietnam War was reaching full force by the end of my second year of art school, and protesting that misconceived conflict began taking on a higher importance than art classes. Through that period and into the present, I worked hard without teachers to overcome my deficiencies. By the early 1990s, some of the best figure-work from my hand of which I was capable began emerging in drawings and paintings. Though still flawed, this one was, I thought, among the best I'd done. But I'm not so good a judge of my own work.

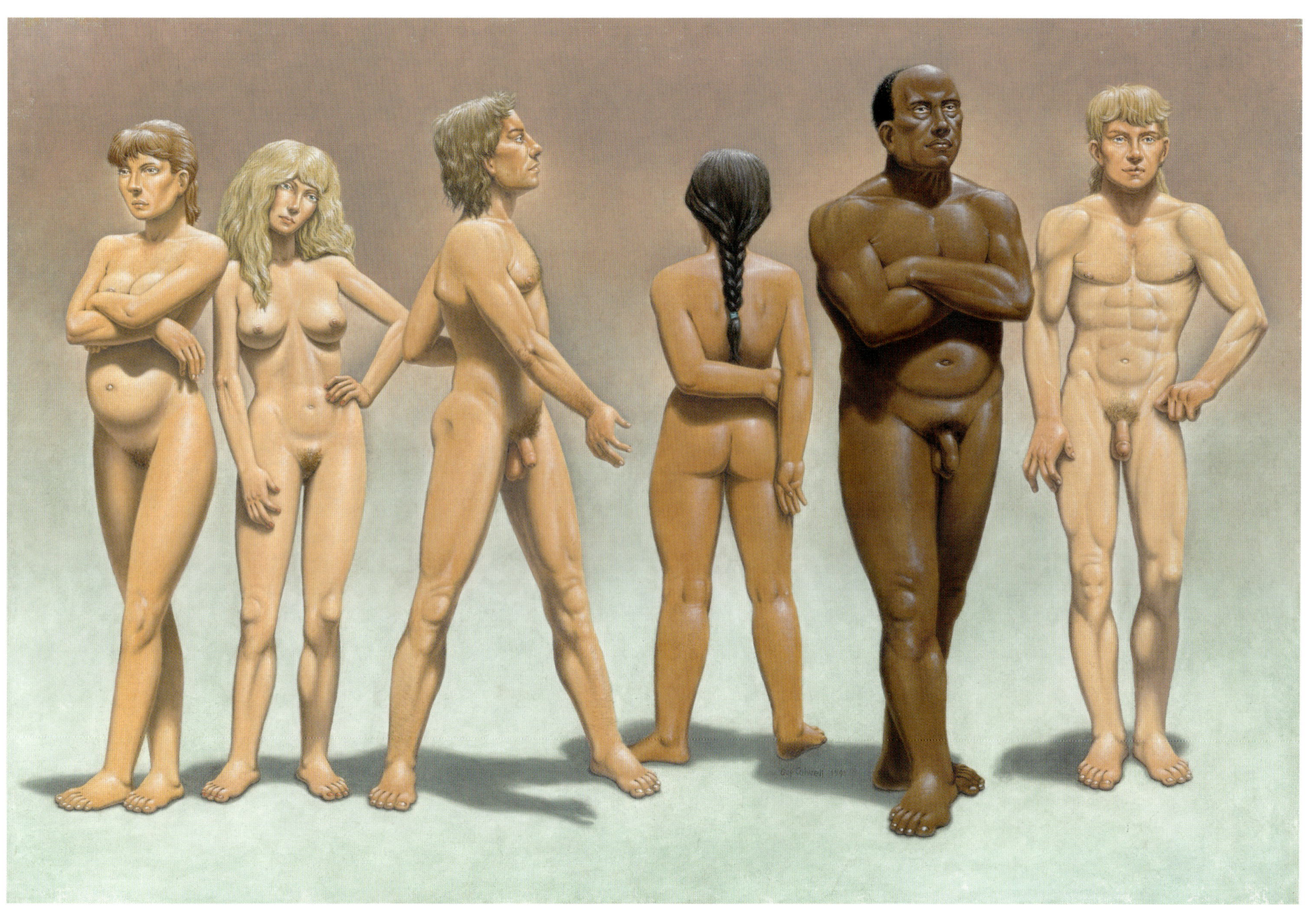

THE ABUSE

Acrylic on canvas • 2004 • 39 × 39 in.
Owned by artist

Abu Ghraib. Something needed to be said. This is not the way U.S. soldiers should be acting. This is not what U.S. policymakers should be permitting. My condemnation of torture took the form of a picture. But somehow, a picture can strike deep — perhaps deeper than words, more immediate, more annoyingly penetrating. This picture provoked threats, dumped garbage, broken windows, physical attacks against gallery staff where it was shown, and went around the world in an Associated Press story, where it was reprinted hundreds of times. A tremendous lesson in the power of visual images.

It was a case of angry right-wingers using assault and property destruction to express their disapproval of anyone criticizing horrendous and unlawful interrogation techniques. I thought of my painting, and the gallery that showed it, as a mirror reflecting back a raw truth in the images we all saw from the infamous detention center. And those who objected struck out at the reflection and tried to smash the mirror.

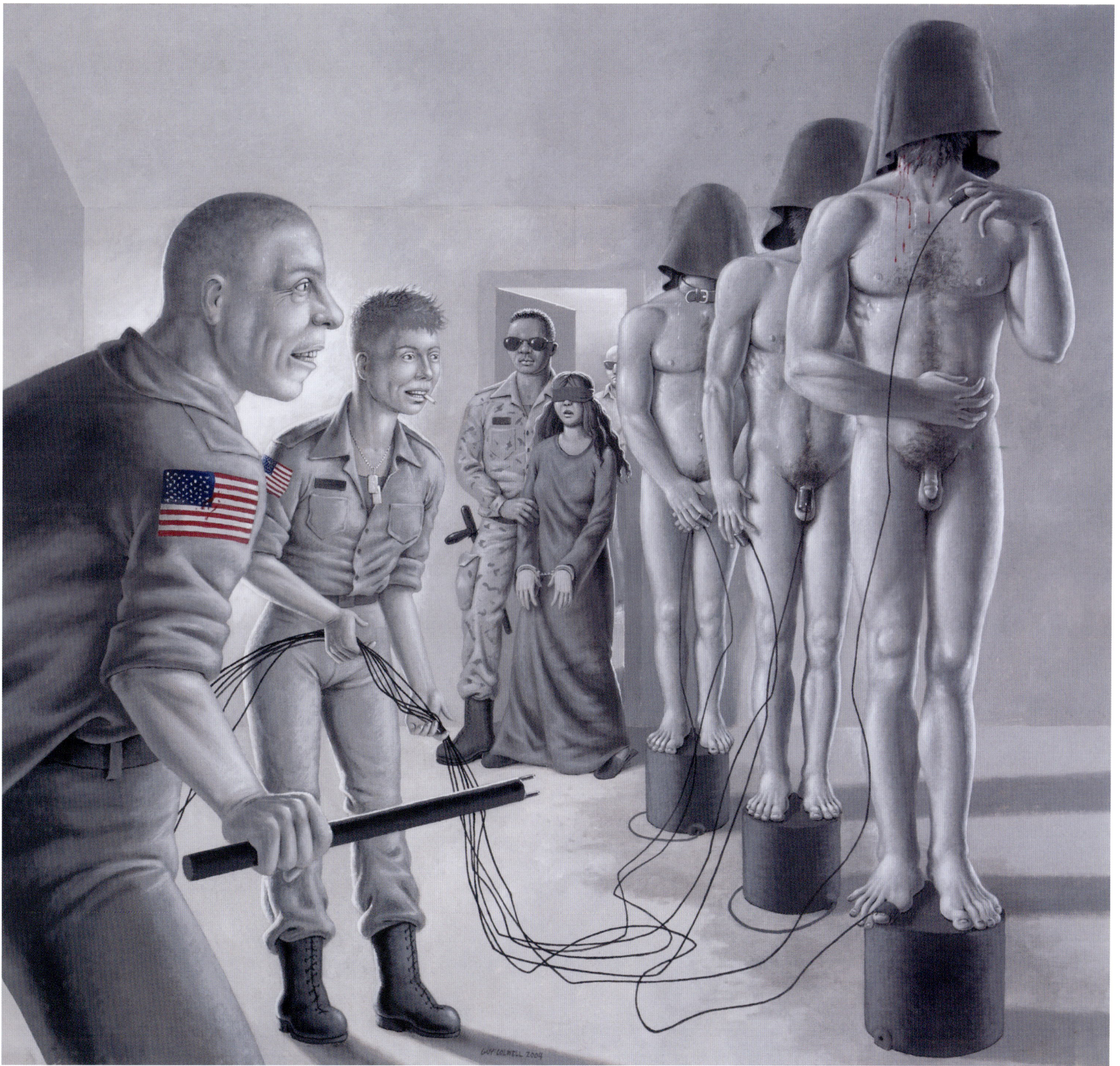

RANDOM DEATH

Oil on canvas • 1992 • 28 × 37 in.
J. Paul Ghetto Collection

The inspiration for this painting came from two sources. First was the ever-present reminders on media that we live in a violent country with men — always men — doing mass slaughter with deadly weapons. The second source was drawn from firsthand visits through zones of massive destruction by fire; one human-caused in the aftermath of the L.A. Rodney King riots; another naturally occurring in the Oakland-Berkeley Hills, 1989, when about 3,000 homes were destroyed. These fires did not cause total destruction. Some structures were still standing when all others surrounding them were totally gone. It struck me how random and patchwork death and destruction can be.

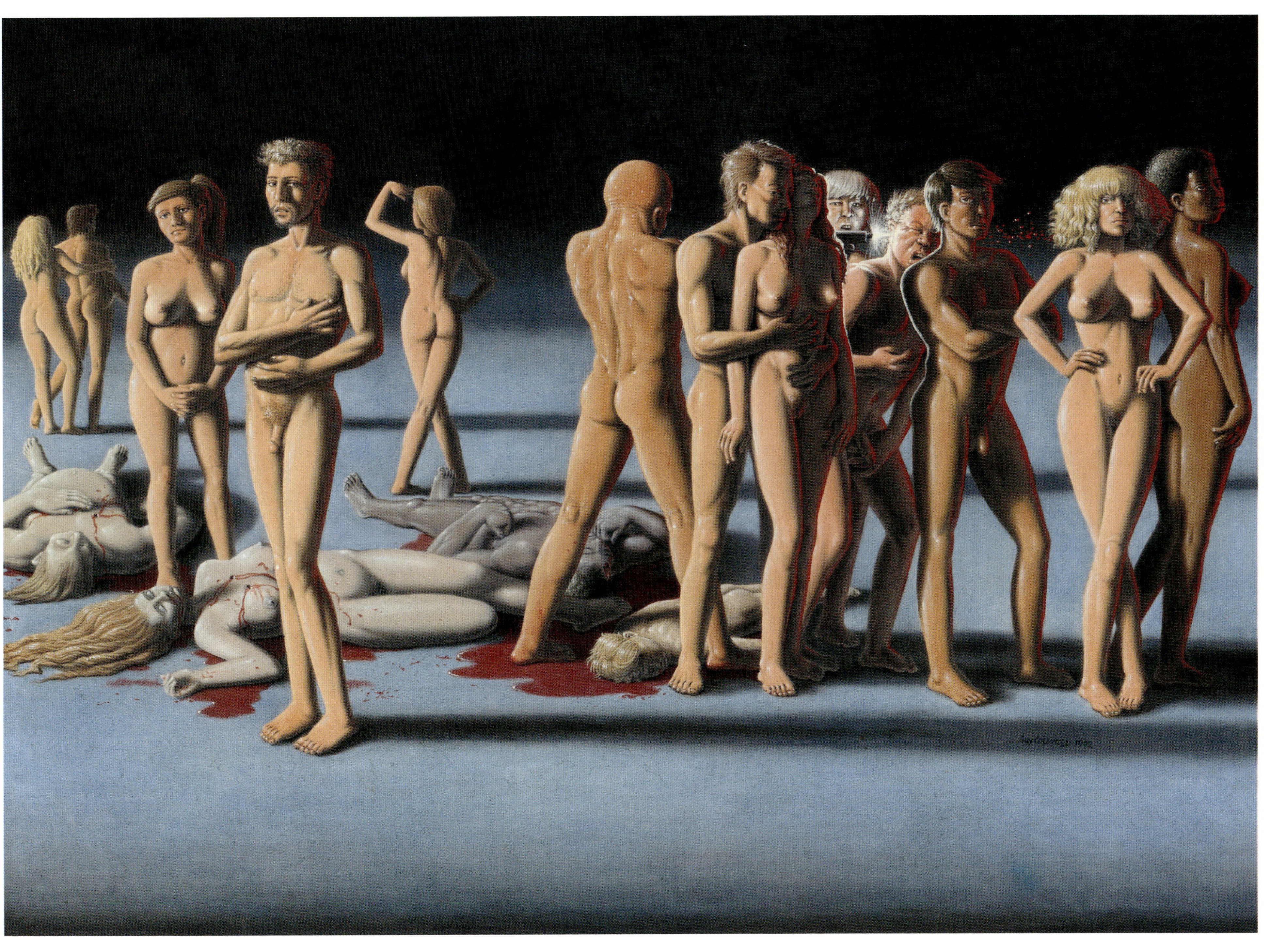

LIST OF WORKS

CURRICULUM VITAE

RECENT EXHIBITIONS

Larchmont Event Space, Los Angeles
La Luz de Jesus Gallery, Los Angeles
Compound Gallery, Emeryville
East Bay Media Center, Berkeley
Unitarian Church, Berkeley
Superchief Gallery, Los Angeles and New York
111 Minna Gallery, San Francisco
Good Mother Gallery, Oakland
Incline Gallery, San Francisco
Pritikin Museum, San Francisco

BOOKS

Inner City Romance #1–5 (1972–1978), Last Gasp
Backwater Babies (1975), Last Gasp
Doll #1–8 (1989–1992), Rip Off Press
Central Body: The Art of Guy Colwell (1991), Rip Off Press
Inner City Romance collected edition (2015), Fantagraphics
Street Scenes (2015), Fantagraphics
In Fox's Forest (2016), Fantagraphics
Doll collected edition (2019), Fantagraphics
Delights: A Story of Hieronymus Bosch (2024), Fantagraphics
Go Figure: Figurative Social Surrealist Paintings (2025), Fantagraphics

SELECTED COLLECTIONS

Alex Seastrom Collection, Los Angeles
Philip Seastrom Collection, Los Angeles
Crocker Art Museum Permanent Collection, Sacramento
Ryan O'Connor Collection, Los Angeles
Jane Goodall Institute, donation of *Primates* by Leonardo DiCaprio
Pritikin Museum Permanent Collection, San Francisco (now closed)
Oakland Museum Permanent Collection
Robert Crumb Collection, France
Felix Dennis Estate Collection, London
J. Paul Ghetto Collection, San Rafael
Jay and Dixie Kinney Collection, San Francisco
Ron Turner Collection, San Francisco
Dr. Ben Teoh Collection, Australia
Hans Grein Collection, Germany
Graham Duncan Collection, London

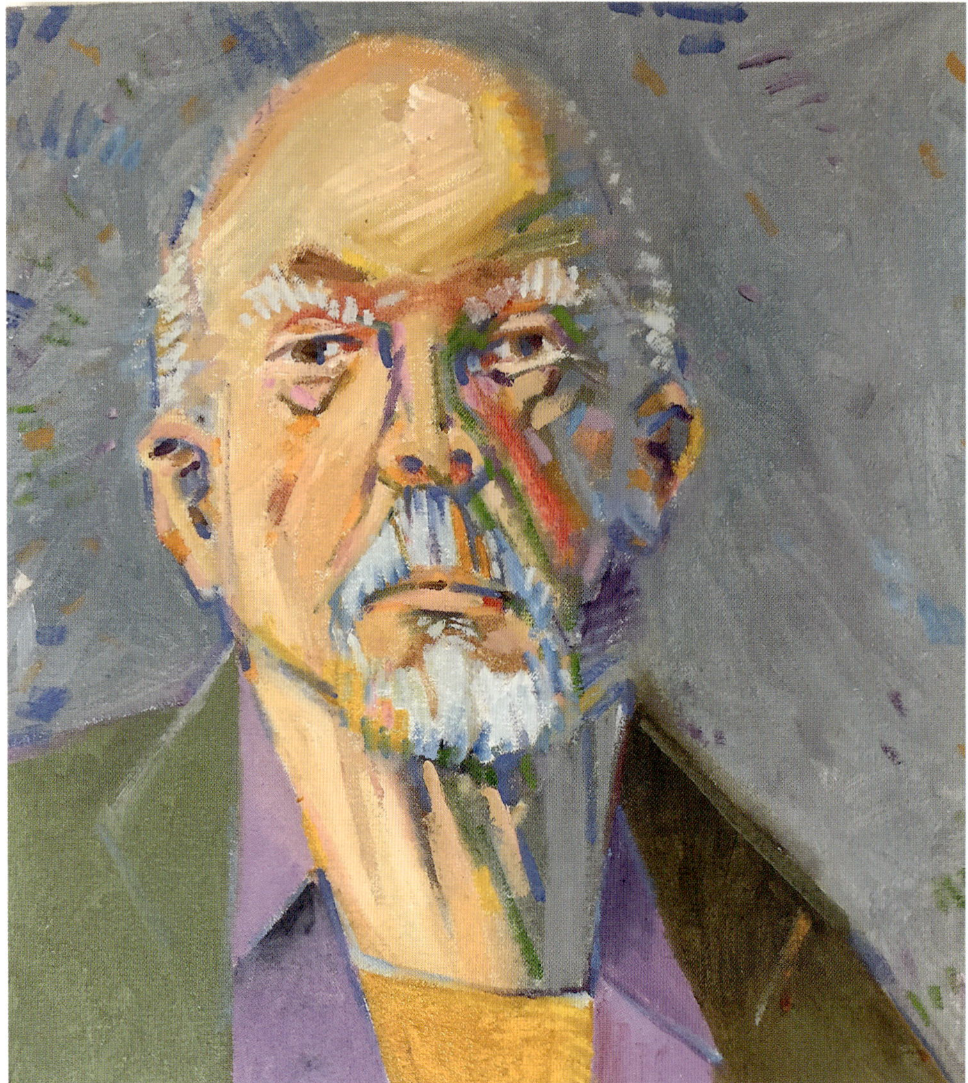

GUY COLWELL, born in Oakland, California, in 1945, is a fine artist, cartoonist and illustrator. He pursued an artistic career from a young age, studying at California College of Arts and Crafts for a stint. A humanitarian, he was sentenced to two years in prison as a draft refuser for the Vietnam War. His experiences in the federal McNeil Island Penitentiary, environmental research travel and activism have hugely affected his figurative social surrealist paintings and radical underground comics, which portray community dynamics, especially in inner-city life. Last Gasp, Rip Off Press, Kitchen Sink Press, and Fantagraphics have published his comics to great (and recent) acclaim. His work is widely exhibited in museums and galleries, on loan from collectors from all over the world. Colwell is a long-time resident of the East Bay Area and lives in Berkeley, California.

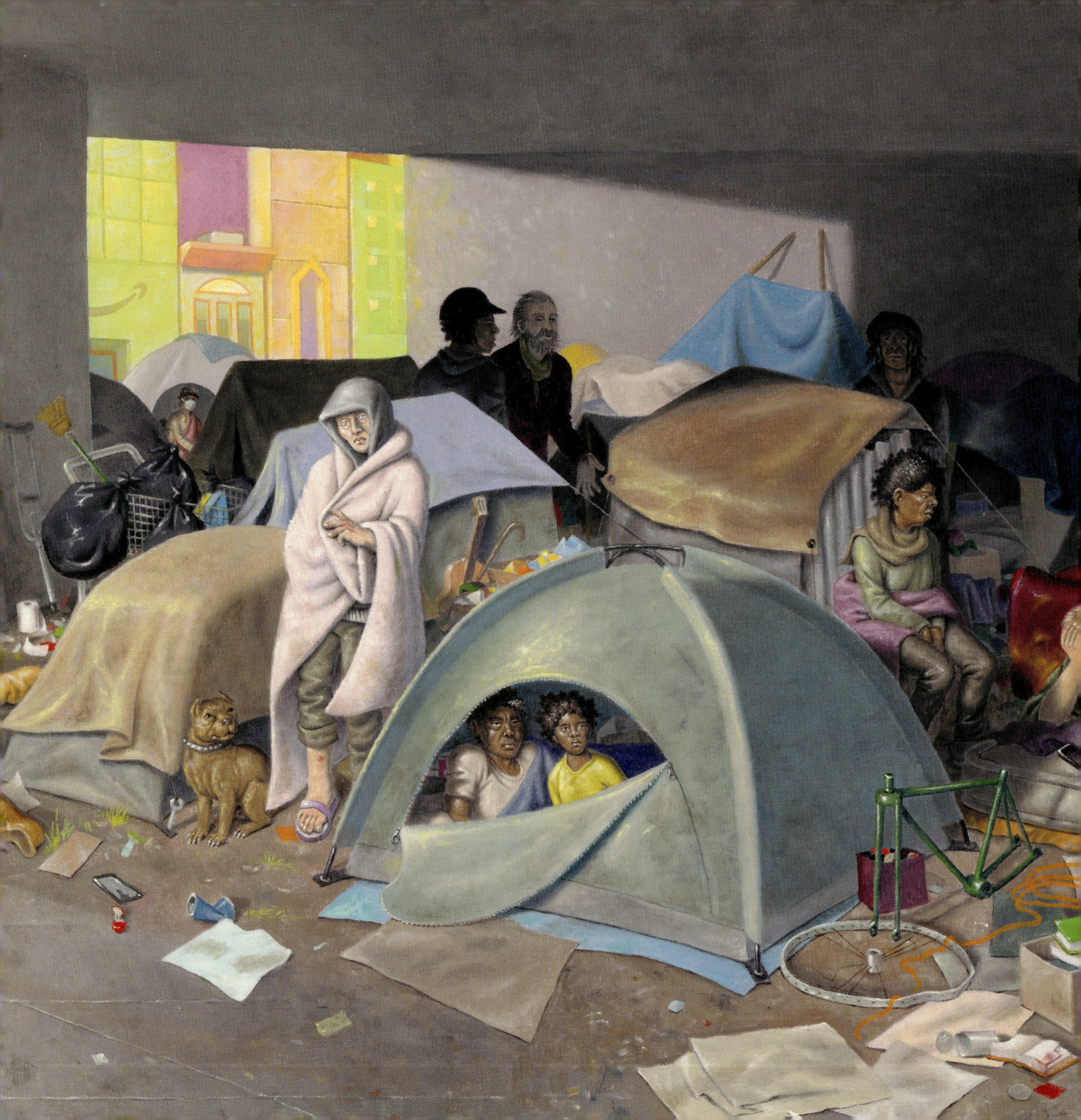